URGENT MESSAGE
FROM A HOT PLANET

Navigating the Climate Crisis

URGENT MESSAGE

FROM A HOT

PLANET

Navigating the Climate Crisis

ANN ERIKSSON

ILLUSTRATED BY **BELLE WUTHRICH**

ORCA BOOK PUBLISHERS

Published in Canada and the United States in 2022 by Orca Book Publishers.
orcabook.com

Library and Archives Canada Cataloguing in Publication

Title: Urgent message from a hot planet : navigating the climate crisis /
Ann Eriksson ; illustrations by Belle Wuthrich.
Names: Eriksson, Ann, 1956- author. | Wuthrich, Belle, 1989- illustrator.
Series: Orca issues ; 8.
Description: Series statement: Orca issues ; 8 | Includes bibliographical references and index.
Identifiers: Canadiana (print) 20210095091 | Canadiana (ebook) 20210095148 |
ISBN 9781459826328 (softcover) | ISBN 9781459826335 (PDF) | ISBN 9781459826342 (EPUB)
Subjects: LCSH: Global warming—Juvenile literature. | LCSH: Global warming—Prevention—
Juvenile literature. | LCSH: Global warming—Prevention—Citizen participation—Juvenile literature.|
LCSH: Climatic changes—Juvenile literature. | LCSH: Climate change mitigation—Juvenile literature. |
LCSH: Climate change mitigation—Citizen participation—Juvenile literature.
Classification: LCC QC981.8.G56 E75 2022 | DDC j363.738/74—dc23

Library of Congress Control Number: 2020951487

Summary: This nonfiction book for teens outlines the science behind global heating and its root causes, provides ways to take action and honors the efforts of the millions of people from around the world working tirelessly to help the planet.

Orca Book Publishers is committed to reducing the consumption of nonrenewable resources in the making of our books. We make every effort to use materials that support a sustainable future.

Orca Book Publishers gratefully acknowledges the support for its publishing programs provided by the following agencies: the Government of Canada, the Canada Council for the Arts and the Province of British Columbia through the BC Arts Council and the Book Publishing Tax Credit.

Edited by Sarah N. Harvey
Design by Belle Wuthrich
Cover and interior artwork by Belle Wuthrich

Printed and bound in Canada.

25 24 23 22 • 1 2 3 4

For nature,
which takes care
of us all.

-CONTENTS-

Introduction

"...the weight of the world is not on anyone's shoulders. Not yours...Not mine. It rests in the strength of the project of transformation that millions are already a part of. That means we are free to do the kind of work that will sustain us, so that we can all stay in this movement for the long run."

—NAOMI KLEIN,
CLIMATE ACTIVIST AND AUTHOR OF *THIS CHANGES EVERYTHING* & *ON FIRE: THE (BURNING) CASE FOR A GREEN NEW DEAL*

The Climate Hub team at the University of British Columbia shares a laugh while describing their mission of climate action focused on justice, joyful community, hope, agency, storytelling and systems change.

VOLUNTEER FOR A community nature conservancy on the small island off Canada's West Coast where I live. Every summer we hire students to deliver science- and art-based nature-education programs to the public. In 2019 I was at a staff meeting in the nature house with our two students, Ben and Caitlyn. Our saltwater aquarium, full of sea stars, crabs, fish and other marine animals, bubbled away in the corner. A three-meter-long (nine-foot-long) humpback whale made out of wire and recycled plastic hung from the rafters above our heads. In the corner, paper bats hibernated in our bat cave, not far from our papier-mâché beehive. Outside, real native bees buzzed from plant to plant in the pollinator garden. Perhaps whales were swimming by just off the beach. We were immersed in the nature I love, but I was distressed. I had just started the research for this book and was having a hard time with the serious *climate* news I was reading every day.

"How should I talk about all these climate disasters with young people?" I asked the students. "I don't want to freak readers out."

"Be honest—tell the truth," they both said. Then they added, "But make sure you also tell them what they can do."

Other youth I interviewed had the same advice. I've taken it to heart. In a few words, borrowed from several sources, here's the honest truth I learned about the climate crisis:

It's real.

It's now.

It's bad.

The experts agree.

It's caused by us.

We know how to fix it.

There's still time!

The more we do, the better off we'll be.

From Grace Nosek at the UBC Climate Hub in Vancouver, British Columbia, I learned that it's possible to use the words *climate crisis* and *joy* in the same sentence. From Swedish youth climate activist Greta Thunberg, I learned that "no one is too small to make a difference." From everyone I interviewed, I learned that action breeds hope and that action taken with others is an antidote to despair. I learned that if we do nothing, we'll end up with what we're currently headed toward—a hot, stormy planet where life is harder for humans and all the other species we share it with. Most important, I learned that we're all needed. Keep that in mind as you read through the next chapters. You are needed!

GRETA THUNBERG IS A CLIMATE HERO!

Swedish teen Greta Thunberg, who started the Fridays For Future movement, has inspired young people from all over the world to strike every Friday to press the adults in charge to take meaningful action to solve the climate crisis.

There's no doubt about it. We messed up. Big-time. When I say "we," I mean human civilization. *Homo sapiens*. The generations and generations who came before you. We collectively lost our way. We forgot that we're part of nature and dependent on ecosystem health for clean water, clean air, food, warmth, every-thing that sustains us. Our use of **fossil fuels** (oil, natural gas and coal) to power our consumer lifestyles, the destructive way we gather raw materials to manufacture all the things we buy, and the industrial methods we use to grow most of our food have ravaged nature, displaced communities and changed the climate, sending the planet's temperature soaring. As a result, many people, maybe even you, have experienced severe heat waves, drought, flooding, violent wind and rainstorms, wildfires or rising sea levels. Lots of people have lost their homes. Many have died. The people least responsible for the problems—children, the poor, the marginalized, and the Indigenous Peoples who live on the land, close to nature—have been impacted the most. We've left you a terri-ble legacy. For that I am sorry. It's not fair. But I want you to know you aren't alone. Millions of adults, including me, are committed to walking alongside you to figure this out while we're still around.

The world's climate scientists agree about the causes of the problem and the solutions. We need to stop destroying nature and burning fossil fuels. We need to do it fast. And at the same time, we need to slow down and stop talking about economic growth. We're in a planetary emergency, sliding down a steep, dangerous slope, and we need to put on the brakes and accelerate in reverse. To be successful we need to take actions that restore nature and improve the lives of all the planet's inhabitants. We need a systems change.

AUTUMN PELTIER IS A CLIMATE HERO!

Water warrior Autumn Peltier from Wiikwemkoong Unceded Territory on Manitoulin Island, ON, says, "My people can't drink oil."

The climate crisis is complicated. It's not just one problem. It's three: global heating, ecological destruction and inequality. When I use the term *climate crisis*, I mean all three. Barry Commoner's first law of ecology states that "everything is connected to everything else." This is what North American Indigenous Peoples mean when they use the phrase *all my relations*—trees, rocks, earth, air, water, plants and animals. This law tells us that these multiple problems are interrelated and need to be solved together. Trying to fix one in isolation might make the others worse. This law also tells us that everything we do has a consequence. It's our choice whether that consequence helps solve these problems or makes them worse.

LET'S SUPPORT ONE ANOTHER!
WE'RE ALL IN THIS TOGETHER!
FRIDAYS FOR FUTURE!
THE PLANET IS ON FIRE!!!

I want to say something up front now about *climate anxiety*, also known as *eco-anxiety*, which is a feeling of worry and dread about the crisis. Climate anxiety is real. It's a normal reaction to the difficult news that comes at us every day and to the uncertainty the climate crisis creates about the future. Many people are feeling it. I certainly do, along with most of my friends. A 2019 poll in the United States showed that most American teens are frightened by the climate crisis. Perhaps you are already experiencing climate anxiety. Some of the stories and other information provided in the pages of this book might contribute to those feelings of worry and dread. If that happens, I encourage you to accept your feelings as normal, stop reading for a while and seek out a family member, friend or counselor to talk with. In chapter 6 you'll find a list of self-care tools people use to deal with their emotions about the crisis.

We've never been in this situation before. No one can predict whether our actions are going to work or how the climate will respond to them. Those are two big questions people are asking about the climate crisis. The third *big* question is, What do we do now? It's a complex question with many parts to it, and it is the focus of this book. What do we do to stop burning fossil fuels? What do we do to help nature heal? How do we come to terms with the changing climate? How do we cope if what we do doesn't work? What can we do as individuals? What can we do together, as families, communities, countries, the world?

No one can predict whether our actions are going to work or how the climate will respond to them.

THE CLIMATE-ANXIETY DOCTOR IS IN

"I STARTED OFFERING climate-anxiety counseling because I didn't know how to talk about my fears of what a changing climate would bring, and it seemed like nobody else did either. I wanted to invite people to say what they're feeling about climate change and see if there's anything they want to do differently because of it, so I built a little booth and set it up in a few different public places around the city where I live. I do it every summer, at least once a week and sometimes more.

"People tell me their fears about undrinkable water, losing plants and animals, having to leave their homes and the possibility that humans may not survive these changes at all. I listen, ask questions and help them connect with ongoing efforts to tend the soil and water, pressure lawmakers about climate policy or fight fossil fuel companies and other polluters."

—KATE SCHAPIRA, poet, essayist, teacher and activist

Urgent Message from a Hot Planet is intended to present possibilities, to help you and the people you care about prepare for what is to come, whatever that might be. I'm going to share examples of how people are coping in their daily lives with the impacts of the crisis and, in many cases, adapting to their new world. Maybe you'll see yourself in their situations. You'll see personal writing, poetry and visual art from other young people who've been affected by the crisis and are working for a better world. I hope you'll feel as inspired as I do. I'm going to share with you examples of how others your age and older are learning to exist on finite planet Earth. Maybe you'll feel compelled to join them in taking up this challenge.

What do we do now? Well, that's up to all of us.

CLIMATE CHANGE AND THE VIRUS

WHEN I STARTED WRITING *Urgent Message from a Hot Planet*, no one had heard of the SARS-CoV-2 virus or COVID-19, the sometimes deadly disease it causes in humans. I was working on the book in the winter of 2020 when the spread of the virus rapidly created a worldwide pandemic that changed life for all of us.

While it's uncertain how the COVID-19 pandemic will affect the world in the long run, it showed us that governments can quickly shut down economic activity, come up with trillions of dollars and massive resources, and cooperate internationally to combat a common existential threat. Hey, world leaders, how about doing the same for the climate crisis? The pandemic showed many of us that a simpler, slower life is possible. It showed us that nature can recover quickly when we stop burning fossil fuels. Some cities saw blue skies, and their citizens breathed clean air, for the first time in living memory. The pandemic also illuminated weaknesses in our economic and social systems—for example, in food and medical **supply chains**, and in the care of seniors, the poor and marginalized people. What the world will do with these revelations has yet to be seen. Back to business as usual, or forward together to a healthier, happier planet? The choice is ours.

- TIME IS RUNNING OUT -

Fourteen-year-old Canadian artist **Glen Woolaver** *grew up in Madagascar. He has a strong connection with animals and loves drawing them. He hopes to have a career that involves both animals and art.*

GLOBAL HEATING 101

A Climate Science Primer

"Unite behind the science."

—GRETA THUNBERG,
SWEDISH YOUTH CLIMATE ACTIVIST

- THE EARTH IS MELTING -

Twenty, fifty
years ago
There was
a lot more snow
But now
the earth is melting
My eyes
they fill with tears
When I think
of all the years
We knew
and didn't change
And now
the earth is m
                    e
                        l
                            t
                                i
                                    n
                                        g

—Maia Lindsay

Maia Lindsay, *14, lives with her family and her imagination in Pennsylvania. She strikes weekly with Fridays For Future.*

MANY OF YOU have studied global warming and climate change in school. If that's the case, this chapter will be a refresher. As a biologist and science writer, I've written about the topic in reports and other books throughout my career, yet I learned many new things while doing the research for this book. More information is coming out all the time about the magnitude, impact and consequences of the climate crisis. Maybe you'll learn something new too. For those of you who aren't sure what the fuss is all about, this chapter is a short introduction to the science. You'll notice that I use the terms *global heating* and *climate crisis* rather than the more familiar *global warming* and *climate change*. I have followed the lead of such organizations as the *Guardian* newspaper and the activist group Extinction Rebellion, which make the effort to "tell it like it is" because they know that language is important and are committed to talking honestly about the severity of the situation. Using terms that reflect reality allows the public to make decisions based on reality.

> The climate system is complex, with many variables and influences.

The climate system is complex, with many variables and influences—more complex than can be easily explained in one short chapter. I have tried, with the help of some generous climate scientists, to summarize the most relevant messages to help you understand what has created the situation we are in, what needs to be done and how best to do it. If you are interested in diving deeper into the subject, consult the Resources section of this book or the references list on the Orca Book Publishers website page for this book.

KEEPING CURRENT

ONE OF THE challenges of writing this book is that important scientific numbers were changing as I wrote and will continue to change in the future. The data for greenhouse gas emissions and warming trends that I have given are those available as of August 2021. If you want to keep up-to-date on the science, here are some websites to check out. Remember, though, that it's not so much the numbers that matter but the direction they are going.

For a summary of carbon emissions and carbon budget:
Human Impact Lab, climateclock.net

For daily carbon dioxide readings:
The Keeling Curve, scripps.ucsd.edu/programs/keelingcurve

For greenhouse gas information and trends:
The Global Carbon Project, globalcarbonproject.org

**For the latest Intergovernmental Panel
on Climate Change report:** ipcc.ch

Why is it important to understand the climate science? Without an understanding of the science, it's difficult to take the kind of actions that will make a real difference. Knowing the science will also give you the ability and confidence to talk about it with others. Atmospheric scientist Katharine Hayhoe, a Canadian who teaches and does climate research at Texas Tech University, tells us that the most important action we as individuals can take is to talk about it. I guess that's what I'm doing by writing this book. Talking to you! And listening!

The Science Not Silence campaign of March for Science urges elected officials to champion climate science and climate action.

PLANET EARTH IS HEATING UP

THE AVERAGE TEMPERATURE of Earth's surface is increasing. Why? At a basic physical level, the amount of energy flowing in from the sun is greater than the amount of energy flowing back out into space. Change in global temperature up or down as a result of the amount of solar energy reaching or leaving Earth can be caused naturally by factors such as changes in solar radiation, a shift in the tilt of Earth on its axis or the amount of aerosol particles in the atmosphere from volcanic eruptions. The temperature rise we are currently worried about is caused by increasing levels of radiation-trapping gases in the troposphere, Earth's lower atmosphere, as a result of human activity. Known as *greenhouse gases*, they include water vapor (H_2O), carbon dioxide (CO_2), methane (CH_4), nitrous oxide (N_2O), ozone (O_3) and a few other trace gases. All have a molecular structure that lets solar radiation from the sun pass through but absorbs and reemits *infrared* radiation, which causes heating.

JAMES HANSEN IS A CLIMATE HERO!

In 1988, Dr James Hansen alerted the US Congress and the world to the dangers of global warming.

A certain amount of naturally occurring atmospheric greenhouse gas, mostly in the form of water vapor, has allowed life on Earth as we know it to flourish. Greenhouse gases act like a blanket wrapped around the planet, pushing the global climate toward warming. If Earth had no greenhouse gases in its atmosphere, the average surface temperature of the planet would be a rather chilly -18 degrees Celsius (°C), or -0.4 degrees Fahrenheit (°F). Too many greenhouse gases in the atmosphere would make Earth too hot for life to survive. Venus, for example, has a carbon dioxide concentration in its atmosphere of close to 97 percent. Its surface temperature is a scorching 450 °C (850 °F). While water vapor is the most abundant greenhouse gas in Earth's atmosphere and has the most significant heating effect, its concentrations are not generally determined by human activity. Carbon dioxide is recognized as the most important *anthropogenic* (human-emitted) greenhouse gas.

Greenhouse gas levels have fluctuated throughout Earth's history. Scientists studying *paleoclimates*, which are climates of the past, have been able to track the concentrations of atmospheric gases over millions of years by studying rock and sediment samples and analyzing ice cores, which contain tiny bubbles of air that were trapped in ice sheets and ocean bottom sediments as they were formed. By measuring gas concentrations in the air bubbles, scientists have been able to see a relationship between carbon dioxide concentrations and Earth's temperature. When carbon dioxide levels decreased, Earth cooled, and if they decreased enough, Earth entered an ice age.

When carbon dioxide increased, Earth warmed up, and the ice began to melt. These natural fluctuations in climate and carbon dioxide levels were the result of changes in Earth's orbit and tilt relative to the sun and happened over tens or hundreds of millions of years.

The Blue New Deal is a proposed plan to restore and protect ocean ecosystems, rebuild ocean economies and include the ocean in climate policies.

Ice cores have shown that since the last ice age ended, about 10,000 years ago during the geologic period called the Holocene, the concentration of carbon dioxide in the atmosphere has stayed relatively stable at 280 parts per million (ppm). That means if you picked a million molecules randomly out of the atmosphere, 280 of them would be carbon dioxide. Modern human civilization developed during this stable period, when the surface temperature of Earth averaged 15 °C (59 °F), not too hot or too cold. But over the last 200 years or so, greenhouse gases in the atmosphere have increased, and so has Earth's average surface temperature.

By measuring ocean heat at various depths, using sensors mounted on floats, the international Argo program has determined that the amount of heat energy trapped in the atmosphere is equivalent to turning on two one-watt incandescent Christmas lights on each square meter (1.2 square yards) of the planet's surface. That doesn't sound like very much, but multiplied across the entire 510-million-square-kilometer (197-million-square-mile) surface of the planet, it is enormous. As greenhouse gases continue to enter the atmosphere, they trap more of the sun's infrared energy and Earth's temperature continues to rise.

A scientist with the National Snow and Ice Data Center works with a section of an Antarctic ice core that will be analyzed for its ancient trapped gases, such as carbon dioxide and methane.

HOW MUCH HAVE GREENHOUSE GAS CONCENTRATIONS AND GLOBAL TEMPERATURE RISEN?

WE'VE KNOWN FOR almost 200 years that certain gases trap heat in the atmosphere. In 1824 French physicist Joseph Fourier conducted research into the atmosphere's ability to trap heat, and in 1856 American physicist and inventor Eunice Foote demonstrated how carbon dioxide and other gases react to exposure to the sun's rays. In 1859 Irish scientist John Tyndall proved the relationship between increasing atmospheric carbon dioxide and what is now called "the greenhouse effect." Almost a hundred years later a young scientist named Charles Keeling started to take daily carbon dioxide readings at the top of Mauna Loa in Hawaii. His first carbon dioxide measurement in 1958 was 313 ppm. As he continued his readings, he discovered that carbon dioxide levels were increasing, with regular daily and seasonal ups and downs through the year. He was, in a way, measuring the breathing of

PLANTS ON LAND AND IN THE OCEAN ARE CLIMATE HEROES!

Earth's natural carbon capture and storage technology, plants draw carbon dioxide out of the atmosphere during photosynthesis to build their structures and also transfer much of the carbon into soils.

the planet. In spring and during daylight, when plants in the northern hemisphere were growing the most and absorbing carbon dioxide for photosynthesis, the carbon dioxide concentration in the atmosphere went down. In winter and at night, with less photosynthesis, it went up. But, on average, the Keeling Curve has climbed upward over the years. Charles Keeling is no longer around, so other scientists with the Scripps Institution of Oceanography are taking the measurements. The carbon dioxide concentration in 2021, averaged over the year, is predicted to reach 416.3 ppm, an increase of almost 50 percent from the pre-industrial level of 280 ppm. Earth's average surface temperature has followed the upward climb of the Keeling Curve. Since 1850–1900, the earliest period for which we have reliable records, the temperature has risen by about 1.2 °C (2.2 °F) and continues to increase. The concentration of carbon dioxide in the atmosphere has been growing by a bit more than 2 ppm per year.

WHY ARE GREENHOUSE GAS CONCENTRATIONS AND GLOBAL TEMPERATURE RISING?

DURING THE *Industrial Revolution,* which began around 1760, we started burning fossil fuels for energy. Currently fossil fuels provide about 80 percent of the energy the world uses. Fossil fuels include coal, oil and gas, which are composed of the remains of plants that have been buried underground for millions of years. Fossil fuels are mainly made up of carbon. When the carbon in fossil fuels burns, it combines with oxygen from the atmosphere to form the greenhouse gas carbon dioxide. Carbon dioxide is responsible for 66 percent of the heating that's occurred since the beginning of the Industrial Revolution and about 80 percent of the warming since 1990. Carbon dioxide stays in the atmosphere for hundreds to thousands of years, building up in greater concentrations over time.

Methane, nitrous oxide and ozone are three other notable greenhouse gases. Methane accounts for about 23 percent of the heating so far. Four-tenths of that is emitted from natural sources such as wetlands, where it is released as organic material decomposes, and the remainder comes from cattle farming, rice

Ralph Keeling, son of Charles Keeling, carries on his father's work by taking daily carbon dioxide measurements at the Mauna Loa Atmospheric Baseline Observatory in Hawaii.

cultivation, natural gas fracking and other methods of fossil fuel extraction, landfills and the burning of biomass. Levels of methane in the atmosphere have increased by 250 percent since pre-industrial times. Methane has a *global warming potential* (GWP) 86 times more than CO_2 over 20 years, decreasing to 28 times more over 100 years.

Change can happen fast! It took only 13 years for the transition from horse-drawn carriages to automobiles, as shown in these historical photos from the New York City Easter Day Parade.

Emissions of nitrous oxide come primarily from nitrogen fertilizers used in agriculture, with smaller amounts from livestock manure. Nitrous oxide emissions are increasing every year. Global annual emissions were 10 percent higher in 2016 than in the 1980s. Nitrous oxide is responsible for about 6 percent of global heating since pre-industrial times. It stays in the atmosphere for more than 100 years and has a GWP 265 to 298 times that of carbon dioxide. Unlike the greenhouse gases already mentioned, ozone has a pungent smell. A naturally occurring layer of ozone in the upper atmosphere protects us from the sun's damaging ultraviolet rays. But ozone formed at ground level, when sunlight reacts with pollution, has a global warming potential far higher than carbon dioxide. However, it stays in the troposphere for only hours to

Sources of global greenhouse gas emissions by economic sector

ENERGY
- 14.2% TRANSPORTATION
- 31.9% ELECTRICITY AND HEAT
- 5.9% BUILDINGS
- 5.7% OTHER FUEL COMBUSTION
- 12.6% MANUFACTURING & CONSTRUCTION
- 5.9% FUGITIVE EMISSIONS

OTHER
- 11.9% AGRICULTURE
- 5.9% INDUSTRIAL PROCESSES
- 2.8% LAND USE CHANGE & FORESTRY
- 3.3% WASTE

Source: Climate Watch, based on global emissions from 2018

days, so its strongest effects are more regional than global, in places with high pollution levels.

Another reason for the rise in greenhouse gases and Earth's average temperature is that we have cut down forests, drained wetlands, plowed grasslands, damaged marine ecosystems and depleted soils. Each of these destructive land-use changes releases carbon dioxide into the atmosphere. But that's not all. Earth's plants and soils are **carbon sinks**, which means they naturally absorb carbon dioxide from the atmosphere for photosynthesis and other biological functions and store the carbon in their structures as long as they remain undisturbed. We have decreased nature's ability to absorb the excess carbon dioxide from the atmosphere, and in some cases we have turned the carbon sinks into **carbon sources**. Evidence is emerging that suggests land-use practices that destroy nature might contribute more to global heating than previously thought.

Greenhouse gas concentrations are measured by the Global Atmosphere Watch (GAW) program of the World Meteorological Organization at a network of stations located around the world. They are measured in tonnes, commonly called metric tons—one metric ton weighs 1,000 kilograms (2,204 pounds). Total anthropogenic emissions of carbon dioxide since 1870 from fossil fuel burning, cement manufacturing and deforestation weigh a whopping 2,400 billion metric tons, also expressed as 2,400 gigatons (Gt). Of this, 40 percent has remained in the atmosphere, 25 percent has been absorbed by the ocean, and 31 percent has been absorbed by the land. How much is 2,400 gigatons? One gigaton is more than the combined weight of 6 million blue whales, the largest animal ever to have existed! The emission rate has increased since 1990, with an average of 42 gigatons of carbon dioxide emitted every year.

ANN ERIKSSON

BURNING QUESTION

HOW DO I TALK ABOUT THE CLIMATE CRISIS WITH SKEPTICS (OR MY FAMILY)?

EVER HAD AN AWKWARD conversation about the climate crisis? Are you tongue-tied when a family member, friend or random stranger expresses skepticism that global heating is real or criticizes climate action? I certainly have been. Fear not—there's help. Websites such as *Skeptical Science* (skepticalscience.com) and *Grist* (grist.org) have all the counterarguments you'll ever need. There's even an entire course at *edX* (edX.com) called Making Sense of Climate Science Denial.

But is debating enough? Wouldn't it be more effective to have conversations that help us understand one another better and maybe start moving in the same direction? CliMate is a chatbot developed by the David Suzuki Foundation that can help you learn how to have those tough climate conversations. The goal is to develop empathy for another person's point of view, find common values and have productive communication. Gleb Tsipursky, author of *The Truth Seeker's Handbook: A Science-Based Guide*, recommends EGRIP, a way of talking with others about the climate crisis that focuses on understanding the **e**motions involved (often fear), identifying shared **g**oals, establishing **r**apport, sharing **i**nformation and providing **p**ositive reinforcement. If you try it, let me know how it works for you.

26

WHAT'S THE PROBLEM WITH WARMER TEMPERATURES?

A **S I WRITE** this paragraph, it's snowing outside my window and the temperature is below freezing. It might be nice if it were a little warmer, but snow and cold in winter are normal where I live. There's a difference between the weather you see outside and the long-term climate, which is the average weather over time. The rise in average global temperature is changing the climate so that the weather you expect to have might not be the weather you get. Summer temperatures above 30 °C (86 °F) are not expected where I live but are occurring more frequently. Global heating is increasing the frequency and severity of extreme weather events such as heat waves, torrential rain, drought and superstorms. Even periods of extreme or unusual cold can occur as a result. Global heating is also causing sea levels to rise.

SEA LEVEL RISE

YOU KNOW FROM BASIC CHEMISTRY (or a pot boiling over on a stove) that when liquids are heated, they take up more space because the molecules absorb more energy and move faster. This is called *thermal expansion*. The ocean is a *heat sink* and has absorbed over 90 percent of the excess heat energy that human activities have created. The resulting sea level rise is not uniform around the globe, but about half of the average rise over the last century is estimated to be the result of thermal expansion. The other half is the result of glaciers and ice sheets melting into the ocean. So far, the average sea level rise since pre-industrial times has been about 20 centimeters (8 inches).

Paleoclimate data tell us that about 120,000 years ago, during the Eemian interglacial period—the last time Earth had a similar temperature to what it is today—sea levels were 6 to 9 meters (20 to 30 feet) higher than they are now. At those levels, my house would be underwater! Luckily we haven't seen that amount yet.

This is because the ocean, with its great volume, has a lot of *thermal inertia.* This means it takes a long time for its temperature to respond to increasing or decreasing amounts of heat. The result is a lag, or delay, in the amount of thermal expansion relative to greenhouse gas concentrations in the atmosphere. This lag means that we haven't yet seen the full extent of sea level rise from past emissions of greenhouse gases. Even if we stop adding greenhouse gases to the atmosphere today, sea levels will continue their upward climb, and efforts to remove greenhouse gases from the atmosphere will take a long time to have enough of a cooling effect to reverse thermal expansion and ice melt.

In addition, if we allow Earth's surface temperature to increase too much now, the great ice sheets in Greenland and Antarctica will melt completely over the next few hundred to thousands of years, slowly adding to the amount of fresh water flowing into the ocean.

Scientists can't predict accurately (yet!) how high sea levels will get or for how long, but paleoclimate studies once again give us a clue. The last time Earth had a carbon dioxide concentration over 400 ppm was during the Pliocene Epoch, three million years ago. The average global surface temperature then was as much as 3 °C (5.4 °F) warmer than in pre-industrial times. Ocean levels were 15 to 25 meters (50 to 80 feet) higher.

GLOBAL WARMING? CLIMATE CHANGE? WHAT'S THE DIFFERENCE?

GLOBAL WARMING, OR GLOBAL HEATING, refers to increases in the average temperature of Earth due to the increased retention of infrared radiation by greenhouse gases.

Climate change is a more general term than global warming and includes changes in Earth's past climate driven by natural causes (such as changes in the tilt of the planet, or volcanic aerosols) as well as ongoing changes due to greenhouse gases. The term climate change refers to variables beyond temperature, such as rainfall, humidity, winds and sea level rise.

REGIONAL WEATHER EXTREMES

JET STREAMS ARE currents of high-speed winds in the troposphere that generally keep weather systems moving across Earth's surface. The winds are the result of the gradual difference (or gradient) in temperature between the tropics and the poles. The higher the gradient, the stronger the jet stream.

As global heating occurs, the poles are getting warmer faster than the tropics. This is owing to something called *albedo*, the reflective power of a surface—a dark surface absorbs more heat than a light one. When referring to Earth's surface, more ice and snow (higher albedo) force the climate toward cooling. More land and water (lower albedo) force it toward warming, which releases more carbon dioxide

Warming oceans increase the intensity of hurricanes, like Hurricane Irma, which caused widespread destruction and flooding in 2017, particularly in the northeast Caribbean and the Florida Keys.

from the soil and water, causing more warming and melting and so on. This process is called an *amplifying feedback*. The rapid increase of carbon dioxide released into the atmosphere as a result of human activity has turned snow and ice melt, once a slow amplifying feedback, into a fast amplifying feedback that is speeding up warming and snow and ice melt at the poles at a rate never seen before.

As the poles warm, the temperature gradient between the tropics and poles is decreasing, making the jet stream currents more sluggish. As they slow, the wind currents form loops, in the same way a circle of cord spun on your finger will form loops as it slows. The result can be regional weather patterns that get stuck in places or occur in unusual locations.

In addition, warm air found above a warmer ocean holds more water vapor, which provides fuel for thunderstorms, tornadoes and tropical storms, producing more frequent storms of greater intensity and longer duration. Every degree of warming creates a 7 percent increase in the intensity of rain events. Slower-moving storms also mean all the rain falls in one place and for a longer duration. Because the sea surface is warmer, tropical storms can occur farther north and with greater strength. In coastal regions, extreme storms combined with sea level rise will result in higher storm surges. Extreme weather has always happened, but global heating is making it more likely and even more extreme.

WHAT CAN WE EXPECT?

AS WE KNOW from Venus and from the study of Earth's climate history, increasing levels of greenhouse gases can make the planet less livable, not only for humans but for all life on Earth. High carbon dioxide levels have been associated with four of the five mass extinctions recorded in the geologic record.

Amplifying feedbacks can lead to **tipping points**, thresholds beyond which large unstoppable and irreversible changes take place in the climate system. Scientists are closely watching a number of potential tipping points in Earth's climate system that they thought were unlikely to occur until the average global temperature has increased by 5 °C (9 °F) or more. Recent reports now suggest some could tip between 1 °C (1.8 °F) and 2 °C (3.6 °F) of global heating—and may already be tipping. These include the retreat of the ice sheets in the Antarctic and Greenland, shrinking sea ice in the Arctic, dieback of the Amazon and boreal forests, slowdown of ocean circulation, thawing of permafrost and die-off of tropical corals.

Scientists have calculated that Earth's surface temperature will increase about 3 °C (5.4 °F) with each doubling of the atmospheric concentration of carbon dioxide. At the current rate of total greenhouse gas emissions, they estimate we'll get to that point between 2030 and 2052, and to 4.1 to 4.8 °C (7.4 to 8.6 °F) by 2100. Current international targets (see chapter 5), if they work, might keep temperature increases at 3.2 to 3.4 °C (5.8 to 6.1 °F) by 2100.

We don't want to get to three degrees Celsius! Not even close. Four degrees is unthinkable. At the current global temperature increase of about 1.2 °C (2.2 °F), we're already seeing serious climate disruption. One way to look at the climate crisis is that it's an urgent message from nature telling humanity we need to get busy and cool the planet down.

WHAT ABOUT CLIMATE DENIERS?

AT LEAST 97 PERCENT of the scientific papers on climate change agree that the planet is heating up because of green-house gases, that it's a big problem and that humans are the cause. What about the other 3 percent who believe global heating isn't happening, or that it's not harmful, or that it's happening but humans are not the cause? Could they be right? The answer is no. A review published in the journal *Theoretical and Applied Climatology* showed that all 38 published papers denying anthropogenic global warming were flawed. The results had been cherry-picked to support the desired conclusions, or the data had been manipulated to fit a desired outcome, or the physics had been ignored. Climate deniers (also called climate skeptics) use these so-called scientific papers, which should never have been published in the first place, to spread **fake news** and get attention for their claims that global heating isn't a problem. Denialism has contributed to the lack of action to solve the climate crisis. Now *that's* a problem.

Author Stan Kozak identified three kinds of deniers. Ignorant deniers deny the facts, either to justify their inaction or to protect themselves against an uncomfortable reality. Interpretive deniers accept the facts but interpret them in a way that lets them off the hook ("my actions are insignificant"). Implicative deniers take the climate crisis seriously but don't do enough or the right things.

HOW TO SPOT FAKE NEWS

CONSIDER THE SOURCE

Click away from the story to investigate the site, its mission and its contact info.

READ BEYOND

Headlines can be outrageous in an effort to get clicks. What's the whole story?

CHECK THE AUTHOR

Do a quick search on the author. Are they credible? Are they real?

SUPPORTING SOURCES

Click on those links. Determine if the info given actually supports the story.

CHECK THE DATE

Reposting old news stories doesn't mean they're relevant to current events.

IS IT A JOKE?

If it is too outlandish, it might be satire. Research the site and the author to be sure.

CHECK YOUR BIASES

Consider if your own beliefs could affect your judgment.

ASK THE EXPERTS

Ask a librarian, or consult a fact-checking site.

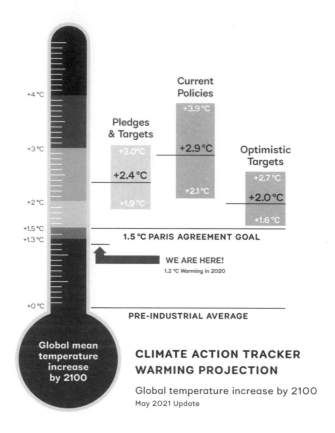

Current
Policies
+3.9 °C

Pledges
& Targets
+3.0 °C
+2.9 °C

Optimistic
Targets
+2.7 °C

+4 °C

+2.4 °C

+2.0 °C

+3 °C

+2.1 °C

+1.6 °C

+2 °C

+1.9 °C

1.5 °C PARIS AGREEMENT GOAL

+1.5 °C
+1.3 °C

WE ARE HERE!
1.2 °C Warming in 2020

+0 °C

PRE-INDUSTRIAL AVERAGE

Global mean
temperature
increase
by 2100

**CLIMATE ACTION TRACKER
WARMING PROJECTION**

Global temperature increase by 2100
May 2021 Update

WHAT'S A "SAFE" LEVEL?

SCIENTISTS OFTEN USE computer models, based on past
(e.g., paleoclimate data) and present (e.g., Global Atmosphere
Watch measurements) observations, combined with a variety
of scenarios and variables to project what might happen in the
future. For example, if we do nothing to stop current greenhouse
gas emissions, a scenario often referred to as business as usual (BAU),

we'll end up with a higher global temperature and more severe impacts by 2050 than if we cut greenhouse gas emissions by half or completely. There are many different models based on different inputs. Some people are skeptical of climate modeling, suggesting it's a form of guessing, but according to a 2020 analysis by the NASA Goddard Institute for Space Studies, many models are proving to be pretty accurate when compared to actual measurements.

We have no time to lose.

The United Nations Intergovernmental Panel on Climate Change (IPCC) is the international body dedicated to reporting the science of climate change and its potential impacts to the world. The IPCC uses several climate models and predictions from various climate labs to compare BAU with other levels of emissions reductions. In its 2019 report, *Global Warming of 1.5 °C*, the IPCC gave an example based on modeling to show that cutting carbon dioxide emissions from 2010 levels by 45 percent by the year 2030 and getting to **net-zero emissions** (as much emitted as absorbed by the biosphere) by 2050 should keep global heating under 1.5 °C (2.7 °F) and limit impacts compared to higher temperature increases. Many people have taken this to mean that 1.5 °C is a safe level of temperature increase, that it should be our end goal and that we have only a few years to get there or the world as we know it will come to an end. The international community, through UN climate negotiations, has accepted 1.5 °C as its aspirational goal. The IPCC's 2021 report estimates that as of the beginning of 2020, the total amount of carbon the world can emit and still have a reasonable chance (50 to 83 percent) of staying under a 1.5 °C increase in global temperature is 300 to 500 gigatons. At current emission levels, that **carbon budget** will be used up in seven to twelve years! But is 1.5 °C a safe-enough goal?

Climate scientist Navin Ramankutty created this sign for a climate strike to remind us that, even if our actions don't stop global heating right away, every bit of temperature rise we are able to prevent will limit the harm.

Paleoclimate data tell us human civilization developed and flourished over the period of the current Holocene Epoch, when the atmospheric concentration of carbon dioxide was relatively stable at 280 ppm and the global average temperature was, at its highest, about 1 °C (1.8 °F) higher than in pre-industrial times. Climate scientists are telling us that the safest course of action is to limit the temperature increase to no more than 1 °C and reduce atmospheric carbon dioxide concentrations to below 350 ppm. We've already overshot both. Our remaining carbon budget is zero—in fact, less than zero. We have no time to lose. But keep in mind, each increment of a degree of temperature rise we can prevent or reverse will lessen the impacts. It's never too late to act. We need to stop emitting greenhouse gases and start removing them from the atmosphere, *yesterday*!

- LIVING IN HARMONY WITH NATURE -

I HAVE FELT deeply in harmony with the natural world for as long as I can remember. Being homeschooled, I have spent much of my time outdoors, observing and connecting with plants and animals. Even though I am now in high school, I continue to learn from and value the beauty and mystery of nature.

As a youth climate activist, striking gives me a chance to think about and enforce my priorities. When I strike, I do it for life, for the air we breathe, for the water that sustains us, for every organism that is alive. I ask for change because I want every natural ecosystem across the globe to be preserved. Striking may not be the ultimate solution to the climate crisis, but it gives every one of us a voice, and each voice deserves to be heard.

Growing up in an environmentally conscious family, along with my own concerns for the living world, has driven me to find ways to make my lifestyle more nature-friendly. Besides recycling, refusing to use plastic bags, and eating locally grown food, I avoid all bottled cosmetics, prefer to walk or bike instead of using a car, and buy most of my clothing and possessions secondhand.

I believe that in order to solve the climate emergency, the leaders of every nation and the citizens of those nations have to unite and work together toward a healthier environment. I also believe that we, the climate strikers, will eventually compel the people in power to take steps toward a future in which there is a stable climate, all countries are carbon neutral and there is equity among all living beings.

—Almila Dükel

Almila Dükel, *16, is a climate activist from Turkey.*

-2-

CLIMATE CHANGED

The Consequences of Global Heating

"...every tenth of a degree of global heating that we can avoid or reverse can help millions of people, millions of children, live better lives, have more choices, avoid more misery, escape a pretty grim life. But also outside our own species, there are at least 10 million other species that we can help get through this period with every bit of change that we make. And for me, that's more than enough motivation to keep focused."

—**PHOEBE BARNARD**, CO-AUTHOR OF *WORLD SCIENTISTS' WARNING OF A CLIMATE EMERGENCY*

Janoš Vranek, *19, is a photographer and passionate climate activist from Aberystwyth, Wales. He hopes his work and words will encourage those around him to change for the better and protect the planet.*

THE CLIMATE CRISIS is not something far in the future. It's happening now, today, around the world. For many of us it can seem hard to fathom the level of the disruption. Our lives generally go on as usual. When I look out of my writing studio and see a calm sunny day and a beautiful oceanscape with flocks of mergansers dabbling about, I can fool myself into thinking there's

nothing wrong. But my research, the news and, more frequently, my own eyes tell me that the crisis is already impacting people and wildlife in dramatic ways.

The stories I heard and read about were painful. I wondered if including them in the book would scare readers too much. Then I remembered my student friends' advice: "Be honest." I agree. It's better to know the truth so we can process the information, understand our feelings about it and act in a way that's based on reality. I've also followed their advice to include examples of positive actions you can take to alleviate despair. Taking action, no matter how small, works. I feel it myself whenever I attend a climate strike, make a lower-emissions consumer choice, plant a tree, get my hands dirty with my friends in our community garden, and even when I work on this book. Everyone I interviewed told me their involvement in climate action, particularly with other like-minded people, helped them feel more positive and optimistic, even joyful. The last three chapters focus on actions of all kinds, and I've sprinkled examples throughout the book of what youth and adults are already doing to make a difference.

In my research I came across a spectrum of opinions about the future, all based on the same science, ranging from the doomsday scenario—"human civilization is doomed no matter what"—to the more positive view—"we can still turn this crisis around." This leaves a lot of latitude for how you choose to feel. As you read through this chapter, keep in mind that no one really knows what the future will bring. We've never been in this situation before. We don't know yet whether humans will act with sufficient intelligence and speed, and we don't know how the complex climate system will respond. Being the optimist I am, I figure as long as there are possibilities, there's hope. That's why it's so important to have up-to-date information about impacts so we know what kind of actions are needed to both mitigate and adapt to the situation. But if you find this information overwhelming, take a break or find someone to talk to about how you are feeling. Come back to it later or skip ahead to the next chapters, which focus on celebrating climate action and finding solutions.

RISING SEAS

A **DECADE AGO, WHEN** my husband and I bought our oceanfront house, the Intergovernmental Panel on Climate Change predicted that sea level rise would be one meter (three feet) by the year 2100. At the time, we believed our home would be safe from flooding for our lifetimes and another generation or two of future homeowners. But with the accelerated melting of the Greenland and Antarctic ice sheets, the predictions have changed. Now we're not so sure if or when our home might flood from a combination of sea level rise and storm surge. Still, we are luckier than

The city of Venice has installed MOSE, a system of 78 flood barriers, designed to prevent the annual acque alte (high waters) resulting from a combination of high tides, winds, sinking land and sea level rise.

some. The small 20-centimeter (8-inch) rise of today is already affecting some coastal dwellers. People are wading through the streets of their towns during extreme high tides in places like Liverpool, Nova Scotia; Miami; Venice; Bangladesh; and the Maldives in the Indian Ocean. As you read in chapter 1, even if we were to stop emitting greenhouse gases tomorrow, ice sheets will keep melting and sea levels will keep rising, flooding coastal areas where billions of people live and many of the world's largest cities are built. At an increase of 3 °C (5.4 °F), the temperature projected for the end of the century if global heating continues unabated, sea levels could rise 15 to 20 meters (50 to 65 feet). Between 1992 and 2020 the Greenland ice sheet alone lost over 4,500 gigatons of ice, raising sea levels by about 13.5 millimeters (0.5 inches). The rate of ice-sheet melt is increasing. Burning all the fossil fuels currently available will melt all the ice on the planet, and sea levels will rise 65 to 75 meters (200 to 246 feet)!

For every inch of sea level rise, six million more people become at risk of flooding. Recent modeling by science and news organization Climate Central estimates that one billion people now live less than 10 meters (33 feet) above current high tide lines and 250 million people live less than 1 meter (3 feet) above high tide. That's a lot of people who could be displaced from their homes as sea levels rise. Seventy percent of the people living on at-risk land are in China, Bangladesh, India, Vietnam, Indonesia, Thailand, Philippines and Japan. Sea level rise isn't a problem that will occur once and then go away. Because of the lag time in the melting of the great ice sheets of Greenland and Antarctica, the ocean will keep on rising. If we take the needed action (see chapter 5), we may be able to slow sea level rise, to give us more time to prepare and adapt.

How can coastal dwellers prepare and adapt to the rising seas? Some cities that regularly experience flooding, such as Venice, are spending huge amounts of money to build seawalls and flood barriers, even though the structures may not be adequate as sea levels continue to rise. The long-term solution is to move infrastructure up and back from the ocean. This means restricting development in at-risk areas and planning managed retreats where necessary. The community of Choiseul on Taro Island is the first town in the Pacific Ocean to relocate because of sea level rise. Authorities decided to move the 1,000 inhabitants to a safer mainland location because the tiny island is less than 2 meters (6.6 feet) above sea level and at risk from rising water and increased storm surges. The massive process to build a new town and move everyone is funded by the Australian government. It will take decades but is a good example of planning ahead.

BURNING QUESTION

WILL HUMANS GO EXTINCT?

NO ONE KNOWS the answer. Even the people at the Centre for the Study of Existential Risk at Cambridge University, who spend most of their time thinking about the issue, don't know for sure. But they are working hard to come up with ways to manage the risks so extinction is less likely. It's true that many people are already suffering as a result of the climate crisis. If we continue with business as usual, emitting greenhouse gases and destroying nature, the climate in some areas of the planet will become too harsh to support human life. Growing food will get harder in many places. The population will shrink. It's possible that human civilization as we know it might collapse, as has happened in the past. But that's not extinction. We know the capitalist system hasn't worked very well for nature and most of the world's population. With the possibility of collapse in sight, we have an opportunity to create a new system. What that new system will be is a choice that belongs to all of us. Rather than going extinct, we could choose to create a new, kinder, more equitable system that works for everyone and everything on the planet. Isn't that kind of exciting?

Some very large cities are facing the prospect of having to move inland. Indonesia is working on a planned retreat of its capital, Jakarta, a city of 10 million people, which is expected to be 95 percent underwater by 2050. One scientist from Miami, where high tides are already backing up storm drains and flooding streets even when the weather is nice (termed sunny-day flooding), recommends moving all essential infrastructure around the world, including hospitals, schools, museums, power plants and landfills, to an elevation of at least 45 meters (150 feet), which is pretty hard in a low-lying place like Florida. He also argues that you can't merely abandon coastal buildings and other infrastructure. Toxic and nonbiodegradable materials need to be removed beforehand to prevent them from polluting the ocean as it rises.

Restoring nearshore ecosystems like coastal wetlands, seagrass meadows and mangrove forests to allow sea levels to rise without damaging infrastructure and to buffer the coastline from storms and erosion may be the most cost-effective natural solutions.

EXTREME STORMS

IN THE SPRING of 2019, Cyclone Idai, followed six weeks later by Cyclone Kenneth, hit Mozambique, Zimbabwe and Malawi. The heavy winds and strong rains caused catastrophic flooding that affected over two million people, killed more than a thousand people and destroyed or damaged more than 100,000 homes. These storms were two of the five worst ever recorded for the region. Hundreds of thousands of people were displaced, and cholera, malaria, respiratory infections and other illnesses increased in the poor living conditions.

Funding for disaster planning and relief is needed to help people impacted by extreme weather events, such as these flood victims in Malaysia.

While it is difficult for scientists to directly link specific storms to global heating, they do know that warming seas mean more energy for storms and that a warmer atmosphere holds more rain. These two factors lead to a greater likelihood of more intense storms with heavier rainfall than normal. Other examples of recent extreme storms are Hurricane Ida, which devastated Louisiana in 2021; Hurricane Maria, which caused widespread destruction in the northeastern Caribbean in 2017; and Super Typhoon Rolly, which hit the Philippines in 2020. Between 1980 and 2017, the economic value of losses from weather and climate-related extremes in the European Union amounted to over 450 billion euros (US$490 billion).

Adapting to a future with more and bigger storms means constructing stronger buildings, improving early-warning systems to allow people to get to safety, and developing and funding better disaster relief.

- A CLIMATE STORY -

MY COUNTRY, INDIA, is facing many problems, like sea level rise, melting glaciers, droughts and floods. In 2013 a very devastating flash flood occurred in my home state Uttarakhand. It washed away many houses, agricultural land and villages. Many animals and people died, and many kids lost their parents, home and everything. I asked my father, who is working for a non-governmental organization working on wildlife protection if I can do something to stop all this. He had a discussion with his lawyer friend, and in 2017 we filed a petition to the Indian Green Tribunal against the government of India for not taking our environment seriously. After one and a half years our petition was dismissed. Now we have taken that petition to the Supreme Court of India.

In September 2019, I, along with 15 other children, including Greta Thunberg, filed a complaint against five countries—Argentina, Brazil, Turkey, France and Germany—under the UN Convention on the Rights of the Child, for not protecting us (our child rights) from climate change. There is an inspirational doha by a great Indian poet and saint Kabir Das: *Finish tomorrow's tasks today, and today's tasks right now.* To save our planet we have to start to act now.

—Ridhima Pandey

Named on BBC's 2020 Top Women list, **Ridhima Pandey,** 14 from, Uttarakhand, India, has been challenging lawmakers in her country to bring about positive change on climate and environmental issues since she was 9 years old.

HEAT WAVES

DURING OUR VIDEO CHAT, Canadian high school student Jessica Liu told me she worries about her grandparents, who live in the Chinese city of Nanjing, where summer temperatures have been reaching over 40 °C (104 °F). "My grandfather has a hard time breathing in the heat, so he can't go outside as much," Jessica said. "They run their air conditioner all the time, which is expensive for them and so outdated and inefficient that it gives off more heat, adding to the problem." Partly because she is seeing the impacts of the climate crisis on people she loves, Jessica has become a climate activist with a youth-led group called Sustainabiliteens.

SUSTAINABILITEENS IS A CHANGEMAKER!

Canadian (Vancouver-based) Sustainabiliteens is a think tank for youth environmental activism.

Rising average global temperature and the weakening jet stream are creating conditions of extreme heat in many places. Over the past few years, temperatures have soared in areas, including parts of Europe, India, Africa, China, Australia and South America. Extreme heat is not just uncomfortable. Temperatures over 37 °C (98.6 °F) can be fatal, especially when the humidity is high enough to prevent sweating (the body's natural cooling mechanism). A study of deaths from extreme heat found that in 2000, 30.6 percent of the world's population was exposed to 20 or more days when the combination of high temperature and humidity reached the *deadly threshold*. People with underlying health conditions and those who are homeless or inadequately housed are especially vulnerable to extreme heat. Individuals can protect themselves by seeking out shade, drinking water and limiting activity.

How can communities adapt to extreme heat? The *urban heat island effect* is the tendency for temperatures in cities to be hotter than those in nearby rural areas. Urban areas contain more heat-absorbing materials like concrete, brick and asphalt, have less airflow owing to the presence of tall buildings, and tend to have less cooling green space. Global heating increases the problem. Using more reflective surfaces in construction, such as white roofs, planting boulevard trees and creating more urban forests, parks and rooftop and vertical gardens are all adaptive solutions.

Some municipalities, such as the City of Greater Sudbury in Ontario have developed heat emergency response plans, which include public advisories and education, water and fan distribution, longer opening hours for swimming pools, the establishment of cooling centers in public facilities and free buses to take vulnerable people to those centers.

DROUGHT

I **WATCHED A SHORT** video made by the World Economic Forum about the Uru people of Bolivia. The Uru have lived on the edges of Lake Poopó, which was the country's second-largest lake, for thousands of years. But in 2014 prolonged drought completely dried up the lake and, along with it, the Uru way of life. The lakebed turned into an empty plain of dry, cracked mud. Millions of birds and fish have died. Even when it does rain, the water evaporates quickly in the higher temperatures. The film pointed out that the Uru survived the Incan Empire, the Spanish Conquest and modernization, but their culture may be vastly and irreparably changed by the climate crisis, as their people leave to find work elsewhere.

Droughts have always occurred, but global heating is making them more common, more severe and longer lasting. Warming air temperatures evaporate more moisture from lakes, rivers and other water bodies. Soils dry up and less moisture evaporates from plants, reducing rainfall even further. When dry land becomes so damaged it can no longer support life, it becomes desert. Climate-induced *desertification* has affected the food supplies, health and income of hundreds of millions of people, primarily in South and East Asia, North Africa and the Middle East. Half of the world's farmland has been lost in the last 40 years to desertification.

Global heating is melting mountain glaciers, considered the water towers of the world and the sources of fresh water for billions of people, livestock, crops and wildlife that live downstream of mountain areas in North and South America, Europe and Asia.

The city of Chennai, India's sixth-largest city, ran out of water in June 2019 after a prolonged drought. Drought is the top climate

These women are working on a reforestation project in Ethiopia, where 15 million acres of degraded land have been restored as part of the Great Green Wall. An African-led movement to plant an almost 5,000-mile (8,000-kilometer) green barrier against desertification and climate change from Senegal to Djibouti, the Great Green Wall will improve the lives of some of the world's poorest people in 20 countries and provide wildlife habitat across the African continent.

change concern in every region of the world. The UN Convention to Combat Desertification predicts that by "2025, 1.8 billion people will experience absolute water scarcity, and two-thirds of the world will be living under water-stressed conditions." The absence of ample, clean water is as big a problem as carbon dioxide emissions. Who can live without water?

Collecting and storing rainwater for use in drought times is a logical way to adapt to increasing drought conditions. My house and many others in my community are designed with cisterns and tanks that collect and store enough winter rainwater from the roof to last through the hot, dry summers. Restoring wetlands and creating water-retention infrastructure such as ponds, rain gardens (depressions filled with plants) and shallow trenches, called *swales*, are natural ways to increase water availability during drought. All living plants transpire, which means they release water as a by-product of photosynthesis. Planting trees and restoring forests can change a dry climate to a wet one.

WILDFIRES

I N THE SUMMER OF 2021, my home province was in the grip of a serious heat wave and drought, with temperatures topping 45 °C (113 °F) in places. The hot, dry conditions set off hundreds of wildfires. Thousands of people, including my friends, were evacuated from their homes, whole towns burned, and hundreds of thousands of hectares of forests and grasslands were destroyed, affecting untold numbers of wildlife and their habitats. Smoke drifted across the country, including into my community on the coast.

Drought and extreme heat create the perfect conditions for wildfires. Although wildfires are natural and important to the health of many ecosystems, the changing climate is making fire seasons longer and the fires more intense. As well, more people are moving into areas prone to natural fire, expanding what is known as the **wildland-urban interface**. The list of regions experiencing extreme wildfires increases every year, from Australia to the Arctic,

Once a wildfire starts, there's not much to do but get out of the way.

California to Portugal, as does the size of the areas burned. The loss of property and loss of lives of people and wildlife increase along with the number of fires. Even wetlands in Brazil have burned. Wildfires act as an amplifying feedback, releasing large amounts of carbon into the atmosphere while at the same time reducing the amount of carbon-absorbing forests and other plants. Of particular concern are the Amazon and boreal forests, which are both critical carbon sinks. A tipping point is expected if these carbon sinks become so damaged by deforestation and wildfire that they become carbon sources.

Once a wildfire starts, there's not much to do but get out of the way. Good emergency and disaster plans and prevention programs are the most important *adaptations* for wildfire. Prevention includes educating people about the natural role of wildfire, encouraging development away from fire-prone areas, managing fuel in and near communities, and retrofitting and building homes to withstand ignition.

MELTING ICE

THE ALASKAN VILLAGE of Shishmaref on the Bering Sea has to move. The Iñupiat people who have lived there for over 400 years are watching their homes collapse into the sea as melting sea ice leaves the shoreline more exposed to storms and erosion. To make matters worse, the ground under the village, a frozen layer of soil, gravel and sand called permafrost, is thawing and shifting. The people of Shishmaref are not alone. More than 30 Indigenous villages in Alaska are experiencing similar conditions and need to be relocated to more stable locations. Without government help, none can afford the millions of dollars it will cost.

Thawing permafrost in Barrow, AK, is causing the town's buildings
and even the graves in the cemetery to shift.

Global heating is not occurring at an even rate around the world.
The increase at the poles has been twice, even three times, the global
average. The albedo effect and changing ocean currents are both
factors. As a result, summer sea ice in the Arctic is melting, and some
estimates say it could be gone by 2038. The loss of sea ice adversely
impacts the lives of northern people, particularly those who rely on
the ice for hunting and travel, and many species of wildlife. The
darkening of the planet's surface, which results in a lower albedo, is
considered a major amplifying feedback in Earth's climate system.

Permafrost covers over 24 percent of Earth's surface throughout
the northern hemisphere, mainly in Siberia, the Tibetan Plateau,
Alaska, northern Canada, Greenland, parts of Scandinavia and Russia.
It is ground that has been at temperatures below 0 °C (32 °F) for at
least two years. In places permafrost can be up to 1,000 meters (3,300
feet) deep. As it thaws in response to global heating, it becomes unsta-
ble and at risk of collapsing, leading to erosion, sinkholes, landslides

and flooding. In some parts of Siberia, land has collapsed to a depth of 85 meters (280 feet). Permafrost stores vast amounts of carbon (1,460 to 1,600 gigatons), almost twice as much as what's contained in the atmosphere. It also stores methane, in smaller amounts than carbon but with a greater warming effect. According to the National Oceanic and Atmospheric Administration's 2019 *Arctic Report Card*, thawing permafrost could be releasing as much as 300 to 600 million metric tons of net carbon, in the form of carbon dioxide and methane, per year.

INDIGENOUS YOUTH NANIEEZH PETER AND QUANNAH CHASINGHORSE FROM ALASKA ARE CHANGEMAKERS!

Because of their activism, Alaska declared a climate emergency in 2019.

The people of Shishmaref and other northern communities have no other adaptation strategy in response to the changing climate but to move. Their homes and livelihoods are literally collapsing before their eyes and under their feet.

IMPACTS ON BIODIVERSITY

B *IODIVERSITY* **IS THE** variety of life in a given area, in all its forms, from blue whales to bacteria and viruses. The climate crisis is affecting species and the ecosystems they rely on in many ways.

Like the koala of Australia, species of all kinds are being impacted by the changing climate. The ancient baobab trees of Africa are dying. Early snow melt can leave snowshoe hares in North America exposed and vulnerable in their white winter coats. Puffins are starving to death in Alaska because the small fish and marine invertebrates they eat are no longer present when they are at their breeding sites. Bumblebees and songbirds are being squeezed into smaller geographic areas as their habitat changes. The nesting sites of tropical sea turtles are vulnerable to rising seas. The Bramble Cay melomys from the Great Barrier Reef in Australia is the first mammal recorded to have been pushed to extinction by human-induced climate change.

SPECIES EXTINCTIONS

IN NOVEMBER 2019, my husband and I watched an online news report about a brave woman in Australia who removed her shirt and used it to rescue a koala from a burning forest. Maybe you saw it too. Bushfires in Australia that year wiped out 80 percent of the koala's habitat and killed more than 1,000 of the animals themselves. Overall, up to three billion animals, including 143 million mammals, 2.46 billion reptiles, 180 million birds, and 51 million frogs, were killed or displaced by the fires. The tragedy became symbolic of the impact of the climate crisis on biodiversity.

Nature is under siege from human activity: changes in land and ocean use, direct exploitation of species, competition with invasive species, and pollution. Human civilization has transformed 43 percent of Earth's ice-free land from forest and grassland to cities and agricultural land, and has fragmented much of the rest with logging roads, seismic lines and pipelines. Half of the planet's freshwater corals are gone. Marine coral reefs may be completely gone by 2030, victims of bleaching (caused by warming ocean conditions), overharvesting, pollution, diseases and land-based and marine development. A fifth of the Amazon rainforest has been lost to deforestation. Even without global heating, we have created an ecological crisis. Nature is becoming impoverished and less resilient. Climate change is making things worse.

The World Wildlife Fund's 2020 *Living Planet Report* tells us that between 1970 and 2016, almost 21,000 wildlife populations experienced an average 68 percent decline in numbers. In 2019 the UN's *Global Assessment Report on Biodiversity and Ecosystem Services* declared that one million species of plants and animals are at risk of extinction, many in the next few decades.

NATURE HAS INTRINSIC VALUE

NATURE HAS INTRINSIC value, which means the land, the water and all the organisms that live on Earth are valuable simply because they exist. Nature also has value for the *ecosystem services* it provides, such as clean water, clean air, food, medicines, culture and recreation, all of which are threatened by increasing temperatures, fire, drought and flood.

SHIFTING CLIMATE ZONES

CARBON DIOXIDE LEVELS ARE increasing at least 10 times faster than ever seen before in the paleoclimate record. As global average temperature rises as well, climate zones in the northern hemisphere have shifted north at a rate of about 60 kilometers (35 miles) per decade since 1970. This is much faster than what is seen during natural climate changes, and too fast for many species to adapt to the new conditions.

As the zones shift, the species that rely on them are also on the move. One study found that over 1,000 species are moving because of the changing climate. Some are expanding their ranges. Other species are getting forced into smaller and smaller spaces, and others are trying to move along with their habitat as it shifts with the changing climate conditions. According to the IPCC, of 105,000 species studied, 6 percent of insects, 8 percent of plants and 4 percent of vertebrates are expected to lose over half of their climatically determined geographic range at 1.5 °C (2.7 °F) of global heating.

Global heating is decreasing reproductive success for some species as a result of earlier spring temperatures, shifts in ocean temperature or sea level rise. They are losing their food supply, their habitat or their opportunities to breed.

Global heating is decreasing reproductive success for some species as a result of earlier spring temperatures, shifts in ocean temperature or sea level rise.

VANISHING ECOSYSTEMS

ENTIRE ECOSYSTEMS ARE FAILING because of global heating. Botanist and author Diana Beresford-Kroeger has described how many trees are dying due to heat stress, lack of water and the spread of plant disease. These include the baobabs of Africa, some between 1,500 and 2,000 years old; Lebanon's biblical cedars; the kauri of New Zealand; and the oaks of western North America. A study published in 2019 by NASA revealed that the Amazon rainforest has dried up significantly over the past 20 years, making it more vulnerable to drought and wildfires. The boreal forest, which captures and stores nearly one-third of the world's carbon, is at risk of die-off. As trees and forests die and their soils are degraded, carbon is released, creating the potential to turn these great carbon sinks into carbon sources.

OCEAN STRESSOR

COVERING OVER 70 PERCENT OF the planet's surface, the ocean is vital to life on Earth. Along with regulating climate, the ocean supports at least two million species, stores most of the planet's fresh water, provides half or more of the oxygen we breathe and feeds billions of people. The ocean and the species that rely on it are experiencing three major stressors at once: ocean warming, deoxygenation and acidification.

Ocean warming

As mentioned in chapter 1, the ocean is a good heat sink and so far has absorbed about 90 percent of the extra heat trapped by greenhouse gases. Critically important ecosystems such as coral reefs and kelp and mangrove forests, normally rich with marine life, are struggling as ocean temperatures rise. Some species can't survive the warmer water and either move or die. As biodiversity decreases, the ecosystem becomes less resilient. Warming ocean temperatures can also cause outbreaks of marine viruses, bacteria and other pests.

Ocean deoxygenation

Over the past two decades, millions of dead crabs have washed up on beaches along the coast of Oregon in the United States. The reason? Patches of ocean with no or low oxygen content. Hypoxia, as the condition is known, is the result of warming ocean temperatures, slowed ocean circulation, and nutrient pollution. Between 1970 and 2010 the dissolved oxygen content in the upper ocean layer, where most marine species live, decreased by 2 percent. The changes are irreversible and will continue at increasing rates depending on how much we reduce emissions.

The consequences of hypoxic ocean conditions are many. Species may migrate elsewhere. They may become stressed and increasingly vulnerable to disease and predation. Dead zones may be created, where marine life can't be supported at all. When the abundance of life in an area decreases, so does the ocean's resilience—its ability to bounce back from extreme events.

These high school students from the Saturna Island Ecological Education Centre (seecsaturna.ca) in the Canadian Gulf Islands are preparing eelgrass shoots for restoration planting by scuba divers. Eelgrass meadows are important habitat for many marine fish and invertebrates, protect shorelines from erosion, and absorb and store large amounts of carbon.

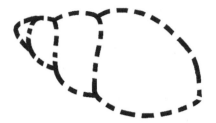

Ocean acidification

The ocean is a good carbon sink. It has absorbed up to 30 percent of the excess carbon dioxide we've emitted, helping to reduce levels in the atmosphere. But increased carbon dioxide in the ocean has another effect. It causes seawater to become more acidic. Acidity is a measure of the number of hydrogen ions in a solution. When carbon dioxide reacts with seawater, hydrogen ions are released. So far the acidity of the ocean has increased by about 30 percent on average, an irreversible change. This is bad news for all the marine species with hard shells and skeletons made of calcium carbonate, such as corals, oysters, prawns and some plankton. The increased hydrogen ions preferentially combine with carbonate in seawater, leaving less for the formation of shells and skeletons. In some places, ocean acidity is already high enough to steal carbonate directly from the shells and skeletons of marine animals, causing their shells to dissolve.

What can be done to stop and prevent these multiple threats to ocean health? Protecting most of the ocean in marine reserves and restoring marine ecosystems will help, but as long as greenhouse gas pollution continues, ocean temperature will keep rising, oxygen levels will keep dropping, and ocean acidification will keep happening. How we can turn the tide on these problems is the subject of chapter 5.

- DEAD CORAL -

Canadian artist **Claire Doty-Housden,** 13, lives with her family on Galiano Island in the Salish Sea. She'd like to share a future with whales, wild salmon and bull kelp.

FOOD SHORTAGES

PEOPLE AT THE World Food Program (WFP) are worried. In its *Global Hotspots 2020* report, the WFP forecast that tens of millions of people in Zimbabwe, the central Sahel region and southern Africa (Namibia, Angola, Lesotho, Zambia and Eswatini) will need food assistance because of severe drought, often combined with conflict and other factors. WFP executive director David Beasley says, "In some countries, we are seeing conflict and instability combine with climate extremes to force people from their homes, farms and places of work ... In others, climate shocks are occurring alongside economic collapse and leaving millions on the brink of destitution and hunger."

Severe weather events, such as floods, fires and storms, and slow-onset events like drought and changing ocean conditions are already affecting food security in many regions of the world. According to one study, food shocks—sudden losses in food production—have been on the rise globally for the past 50 years, particularly in South Asia, the Caribbean, eastern Europe and South America. Climate-related crop failures are also reported in some parts of North America.

Agriculture (crops and livestock), fisheries and aquaculture are all being affected by extreme weather. People are losing their food supply and their livelihoods, particularly disadvantaged and vulnerable populations, some Indigenous Peoples and local communities dependent on agriculture. One study concluded that 90 percent of the world's population—mostly in poor countries where the infrastructure is often more vulnerable to hazards—faces food shortages if changes in climate are allowed to continue. As food production declines, prices rise and the potential for conflict increases. Because the food supply has been globalized, the collapse of food production in one location can have cascading effects all over the world.

IMPACTS ON HUMAN HEALTH

I **N NORTHERN RUSSIA** in 2012, a 12-year-old boy died and over 70 members of his nomadic tribe were hospitalized when they were exposed to deadly anthrax bacteria released from thawing permafrost. This is one example of how the climate crisis is affecting human health. The *Lancet* Countdown, an independent global program, monitors worldwide health in relation to the changing climate. Impacts include heat stress, respiratory disease, heart disease, digestive illnesses, physical trauma and death, adverse birth outcomes, deteriorating mental health and zoonotic diseases (transmitted from animals to humans) such as Zika virus, Lyme disease, rabies, avian flu and West Nile fever. Extreme heat, air and water pollution, food scarcity, and displacement are all made worse by the climate crisis. Children, the poor, the elderly and those with underlying medical conditions are especially vulnerable.

All United Nations member states adopted these 17 Sustainable Development Goals in 2015 as a call to action to achieve them worldwide by 2030.

Source: un.org/sustainabledevelopment/ The content of this publication has not been approved by the United Nations and does not reflect the views of the United Nations or its officials or Member States.

In its 2020 publication about health and climate change, the *Lancet* Countdown reported, among other impacts, over 475 million additional exposures of vulnerable populations to heat waves in 2018, increases in 114 countries to exposure to high-risk wildfires, and increasing transmission of infectious disease such as malaria and dengue fever.

MASS MIGRATION

THE CLIMATE CRISIS is causing people to move too. In 2019 a record high of 24.9 million people were internally displaced (forced to leave their homes and relocate within their home-country borders) by weather-related disasters, most sudden disasters such as storms and floods. When displacement results from slow-onset disasters like drought, the migration can be difficult to differentiate from voluntary migration, such as for work or family reasons. Some *internally displaced persons (IDPS)* are able to return home once things return to normal, but millions are forced to find permanent shelter elsewhere. The people most at risk of displacement are the poor, because they often live in substandard conditions and lack the resources to travel to safety or protect their homes when disaster strikes. Forty percent of IDPS are children. Increasingly, people are having to leave their homes and communities because they cannot feed their families. The World Bank estimates that by 2050 climate disruption will have internally displaced over 140 million people.

Climate migrants forced to cross borders can face life-threatening circumstances and be met with resistance at borders. To make matters worse, climate migrants don't qualify as *refugees* under any internationally accepted treaty in the way that people displaced by war, conflict and political persecution do. This means they do not have the same rights and may not receive even basic help.

Where will all the climate migrants go, and how will they be received?

CONFLICT

THE DISPLACEMENT OF people by the climate crisis, both internally and across borders, is sparking conflicts. In 2016 my husband and I joined with other people in our community to sponsor the Kaiyalis family, refugees from Syria. Zaki, Muzna, Rama and Farouk came to Canada from Lebanon, after fleeing civil war in their home city of Aleppo in 2011. Some experts on the subject believe that agricultural failure, caused by climate change–induced drought, spurred mass migration from rural areas of Syria to the cities, which contributed, along with other socioeconomic problems, to the outbreak of civil war.

Peter Mauer, head of the International Committee of the Red Cross, stated in a 2018 interview with the *Guardian Australia*, "When [populations] start to migrate in big numbers it leads to tensions between the migrating communities and the local communities. This is very visible in contexts like the Central African Republic, like Mali and other places."

Armed conflict is also a contributor to the climate crisis. During my interview with Mary-Wynne Ashford, former co-president of International Physicians for Prevention of Nuclear War, she called the military contribution to the climate crisis its "bootprint."

BURNING QUESTION

WHAT DO WE DO ABOUT ALL THE CLIMATE MIGRANTS?

MUCH HAS BEEN said about former US president Donald Trump's efforts to build a border wall between the United States and Mexico to prevent passage by migrants from the south, many of whom are fleeing drought and food shortages in their home countries. Physical walls and fences are one way to deal with migration. There are currently over 70 border walls or fences in the world today, mostly to keep people out. One of the most recent, the UK-funded mile-long wall at Calais, France, was built to stop migrants from accessing the Channel Tunnel to travel to Britain. Policies to restrict immigration are a form of border wall. But isn't there another way, particularly since hundreds of millions of people are predicted to be displaced as a result of the climate crisis? How about removing the barriers and welcoming the migrants instead?

Several villages in Italy are doing just that. The small village of Riace in Calabria, for example, has welcomed asylum seekers since 1998, many of whom crossed the Mediterranean Sea from Africa in small, precarious boats. The resettlement program offers housing, Italian classes, schools, jobs, food vouchers and, most important, friendship. The benefits are not one-sided. The village, whose population had been dwindling over the years as people left to find work, has been revitalized.

Which story resonates with you? Walls and fences or welcome centers? The climate crisis will eventually touch everyone. Sea level rise is already displacing people in well-to-do coastal communities in the United Kingdom and United States. Think about it. You or someone you love may be a climate migrant one day too.

French street artist JR installed a giant painting of a child named Kikito on the Mexican side of the US-Mexican border to protest the building of the wall. To celebrate the launch of the painting, people from both sides of the border joined together for a festive potluck dinner.

The military is not required to report emissions as part of international climate change agreements. But according to one estimate by Scientists for Global Responsibility, the military system generates up to 6 percent of the world's greenhouse gases. The US military uses an estimated one million barrels of oil a day! Then there's the environmental damage from weapons testing; the effects of bombs and chemicals on citizens, wildlife and ecosystems; and the abandoning of land mines (not to mention the loss of human lives). The US military is a big player in securing oil and energy supplies through armed intervention. In fact, the Transnational Institute describes it as a "central pillar of the global fossil fuel economy."

SOCIETAL BREAKDOWN

INCREASING FOOD SHORTAGES, natural disasters, negative health impacts, displacement and conflict suggest that unless we take drastic action to address the climate crisis and prepare for all these challenges in a planned, humanitarian way, we are headed for catastrophe. Jem Bendell, a professor of sustainability at the University of Cumbria in the United Kingdom, wrote a paper for his colleagues called *Deep Adaptation: A Map for Navigating Climate Tragedy*, in which he outlines evidence to support his conclusion that the world will experience slow-onset societal collapse in the near term (within 10 years), brought on by all the factors discussed in this chapter plus a few others. The others include disruptions in banking and insurance, food distribution, the electrical grid and other necessary services.

Not everyone agrees with Bendell's conclusion or his predicted timeline, but his main message is that it would be wise to prepare just in case, in a way that will ensure peace rather than conflict. He recommends that individuals, families, communities and governments work through four questions he refers to as the 4 Rs of deep adaptation.

Resilience asks, "How do we keep what we really want to keep?"

Relinquishment asks, "What do we need to let go of in order to not make matters worse?"

Restoration asks, "What can we bring back to help us with the coming difficulties and tragedies?"

Reconciliation asks, "With whom and with what can I make peace to lessen suffering?"

It's an interesting exercise. I recommend trying it. Much of this book attempts to answer those four questions. Whether you believe we're heading for societal collapse or not, we do know things are going to get more difficult for everyone. The deep-adaptation agenda seems like a smart and compassionate way to head into it.

CONGRATULATIONS!

IF YOU ARE reading this paragraph, you've made it through a lot of bad news. I hope you feel informed about the task ahead of us as global citizens to tackle the climate crisis for ourselves, our loved ones, the rest of humanity and all the other species we share the planet with. Remember, if we do nothing, we'll end up where we're going. That brings up the question, Where is it that we need to go instead? Looking into the past at the root causes of our situation can help us answer that question.

-3-

HOW WE GOT HERE

The Root Causes of the Climate Crisis

"It's not about carbon: it's about *capitalism*."

—NAOMI KLEIN,
AUTHOR, SOCIAL ACTIVIST AND FILMMAKER

- THEY WILL LISTEN -

Global capitalism the **religion of the individual** smashing through the vision of a united society. **THE CORRUPTION OF THE CURRENT SYSTEM HAS LED TO THE DESTRUCTION OF THE ECO SYSTEM**

But **they** don't agree

When will they listen? **When will they act?** When will they stop selling our future off to fossil fuel companies who don't give a crap?

We shouldn't be here; we should be in school dreaming up our careers, **our beautiful future we watch disappear.**

Instead we take to the streets. We stand strong together. **We fight the deniers, the ignorant, the shameless.** We make our demands and we educate for the nameless.

WE ARE THE FUTURE. AND THEY WILL LISTEN.

—Teän Warren

Teän Warren is a 13-year-old queer youth climate activist from Cornwall, UK. She's passionate about justice within society, our effects on the natural world, raising questions and investigating privileges and prejudices and how they shape the world we live in. Teän is part of the Cornwall Youth Climate Alliance (CYCA) and organises and attends the strikes, where she performs her spoken word poem to the crowds.

'M NOT AN economist or a political scientist, so I was daunted by this chapter about the root causes of the climate crisis. But as I worked through the research materials, I realized the importance of understanding how we got to this illogical place where we have managed to destroy much of the natural world that we rely on for, well, our lives. I came to appreciate how this knowledge is critical to figuring out how to fix the mess we've made—or at least keep it from getting worse.

Greenhouse gas pollution, global heating, climate change, deforestation, desertification, sea level rise, superstorms and ocean acidification are not causes of our current problems. They are symptoms of our ways of thinking and acting that separate us from nature. This separation led us to see nature as existing for our own use. The climate crisis is an opportunity to relearn how to live harmoniously with each other as part of nature and within the ecological limits of the planet. It's an opportunity to understand that there are alternative worldviews to those that got us into the climate crisis, ones that can help us get out of it.

This chapter covers many complex concepts in brief. If you are interested in exploring these topics further, some particularly helpful books are Ronald Wright's *A Short History of Progress*, Naomi Klein's *This Changes Everything: Capitalism vs the Climate*, Paul Mason's *Postcapitalism: A Guide to Our Future* and Charles Eisenstein's *Climate: A New Story*. I'm not going to delve into human psychology and the much-discussed controversies about whether we are naturally programmed to be greedy and violent or cooperative and generous. I'm also going to leave religion alone, other than to say that some religious philosophies contribute to the notion of human domination over nature. I am going to start with us, the human population.

BURNING QUESTION

SHOULD I HAVE CHILDREN?

REPRODUCING IS A vital part of the basic biology of every living thing. After all, without reproduction, I wouldn't be writing this, and you wouldn't be reading it. We wouldn't have a climate crisis either. Humans have developed the technology to make reproduction a choice. That choice is a very personal one. I know people from my generation who decided to remain childless for environmental reasons. In light of the climate crisis, many young people now are choosing not to have children. They make the choice because of the uncertainty and adversity that the climate crisis might bring and/or because they want to make a political statement.

There's no right or wrong choice. Both options can be difficult.

CHILDFREE BY CHOICE

The women-led network Conceivable Future in the United States formed to bring awareness to the relationship of the climate crisis to reproductive justice. It fights for women's right to make reproductive choices free from government-supported harm. It does not advocate for population controls, which have often been used as a form of colonial violence. It supports any reproductive choice a person makes.

POPULATION

FOR MOST OF our time on Earth, about 250,000-plus years, our species, *Homo sapiens*, lived in small groups as hunter-gatherers. We ate the plants and animals that lived close by, or we moved with the seasons to find food and water. Our impact on nature was relatively small, although not zero. For example, about 10,000 years ago overhunting of wooly mammoths by prehistoric humans, combined with a changing climate, is believed to have wiped the large herbivores off the face of the planet.

Populations grew. Waste built up. Local resources became scarce.

The introduction of agriculture, which developed independently in several regions over 10,000 years ago, is thought to be the real starting point of our ecological problems. People settled down in one place, cleared land for growing crops and grazing animals, and had more children to help in the fields or with the animals. Populations grew. Waste built up. Local resources became scarce. Our impact on nature became greater. In his book *A Short History of Progress*, historian Ronald Wright describes how some early civilizations, for example the Sumerians in ancient Mesopotamia (modern-day Iraq and Kuwait), disappeared in large part because of their impact on the environment. Deforestation and other land-use changes led to reduced rainfall, which affected their ability to grow food and sustain themselves. These civilizations had outgrown the **carrying capacity** of the place where they lived. Carrying capacity is an ecological term that applies to all species. It's the maximum population of a species that the surrounding environment can sustain indefinitely with air, water, food, habitat and other necessities.

When I was born in the 1950s, the world population was about 2.5 billion. When my daughter was born in the 1990s, it was 5.2 billion. Today it's about 7.8 billion and projected to grow to over 9 billion by 2050. The *ecological footprint*, which refers to the amount of resources (food, water, land, etc.) the current global population uses, has been calculated to be one and a half times what the planet can provide. If everyone lived a North American consumer lifestyle, the human ecological footprint would be four and a half times the planet's resources or more. These numbers tell us that we have outgrown the planet's carrying capacity. We've also managed to reduce its carrying capacity by destroying and polluting sources of food, water, air and other necessities.

There's lots of debate about whether there are too many people. Some argue that if resources were more equitably distributed, the planet could support 11 billion people or more. But at what cost to the environment? Each person requires land, food, water and shelter at a basic minimum. All those resources come from nature, and all those people produce waste, including greenhouse gases. Whether you live in a grass hut or a mansion, you will have an impact, although some impacts are a lot greater than others.

Another way to look at population relates to the people who live in those mansions. A 2015 report by Oxfam showed that the richest 10 percent of the world's population produces half of the global greenhouse gas emissions. The more money you have, the more resources you tend to consume, and the greater your *carbon footprint*. Rich people live in every country, including developing countries like China and India. Even those of us considered middle-class in

As the world's population grows, the more our collective ecological footprint grows too.

North America and Europe are rich compared to the majority of the world's population. I might have a smaller ecological footprint than my neighbor but a bigger one than my cousin.

These arguments tell us that having fewer people would help, but having fewer rich people would help even more. However, it's not that simple. It's been shown that as standard of living increases and women become more educated, they have fewer children. In fact, the 10-year rate of global population growth has slowed by half, from about 22 percent in the 1960s to less than 11 percent in the 2010s, as *globalization* has lifted millions of people out of poverty and more women and girls now have access to education and birth control. By 2050 the projected rate of population growth will be about 5 percent. These factors have implications for how to allocate responsibility for lowering greenhouse gases and healing the planet in an equitable way, something I'll talk about in chapter 5. Now back to human history.

Indigenous Peoples in Brazil, like these protesters in São Paulo in 2015, have fought for decades to have their traditional land, much of it in the Amazon, formally recognized by the Brazilian government in a way that protects their cultural and environmental rights and their right to self-determination.

COLONIALISM, IMPERIALISM AND EXTRACTIVISM

SOME EARLY CIVILIZATIONS were able to reach beyond their local resource limitations by traveling over water or land to find new sources of food and other material goods, obtaining them through trade or by force. *Colonialism*, the process of exploration, conquest, settlement and exploitation of large parts of the world, increased exponentially around the year 1500 when Portugal, Spain, the Dutch Republic, France and England entered the scene. Colonization was a global land-and-resources grab of massive proportions.

INTERSECTIONALITY AND CLIMATE JUSTICE

THE TERM *INTERSECTIONALITY* was new to me until recently, although the concept wasn't. It refers to the way different forms of systemic discrimination (such as racism, sexism and classism) overlap (intersect) to create a unique experience for an individual or group. It's about the level of privilege some people have because of who they are. People of Color, Indigenous people, children, women, the poor, and disabled people have borne the brunt of both resource extraction and climate-related disasters, even though they are often the least responsible for them. For example, People of Color living in poor communities in Manhattan received less disaster relief (if any) following Hurricane Sandy than wealthier, primarily white neighborhoods did. Climate solutions can suffer the same biases. For example, wind turbines, which can be noisy, might be installed beside poor communities because wealthier neighborhoods have the resources to organize politically to refuse them. The Climate Justice Alliance brings communities on the front lines of the climate crisis together to ensure that the issues of gender, race and class are at the center of decision making about solutions.

The lands the colonizers encountered were not empty, but were inhabited by hundreds of millions of Indigenous people with cultures as rich and old as the cultures of the colonizers. To legitimize the claiming of these territories as their own (a policy known as *imperialism*), European monarchs created the Doctrine of Discovery, which declared Indigenous Peoples to be nonhuman and their lands, therefore, vacant and available. The doctrine was used to justify the killing, displacement and enslavement of Indigenous Peoples by the colonizers, who also brought diseases such as smallpox to which the Indigenous populations had no immunity. In North America, Indigenous populations were reduced to about one-tenth of what they were precontact. The colonizers didn't simply steal the land: they cut down, dug up and fished out the bounty they found there and shipped lumber, minerals, fish and other natural resources back to Europe, without regard for the damage being done. This economic system of taking from nature without giving back has been called *extractivism*. Sound familiar?

Europeans came in great numbers to the "new world" to settle the "empty" land, clearing forests to build towns and grow food. As their numbers grew, so did their impact on nature. In her book *This Changes Everything*, Naomi Klein describes how imperialism, colonialism and extractivism nurtured the dangerous beliefs still in existence today: that other places are for the taking, that if someone is in the way of what you want, you remove them or "sacrifice" their well-being, and that once you've taken all there is, there's always somewhere else to exploit.

PROFESSOR OF BIOLOGY
WANGARI MAATHAI IS A CLIMATE HERO!

She won the Nobel Peace Prize for starting the Green Belt Movement, which empowers women to protect and restore the environment of Kenya and their livelihoods by planting trees. The movement has planted over 51 million trees in Kenya since 1977.

IT TAKES ROOTS TO GROW THE RESISTANCE

IT TAKES ROOTS is a multiracial, multicultural, multigenerational alliance of networks and alliances representing over 200 organizations and affiliates in over 50 states, provinces, territories and Indigenous lands in the United States and Canada. It is led by women, gender-nonconforming people, People of Color and Indigenous Peoples. It works for justice in the areas of race, gender, housing, environment, energy and climate in order to advance regenerative economies and healthy communities.

- MY BROWN VOICE ON THE CLIMATE CRISIS -

I WAS BORN IN JERUSALEM, a city plagued by constant political conflict. I saw the suffocating impact that smog, excess carbon emissions and droughts have on a population—especially one of suppressed socioeconomic status. There, children wake up feeling like they cannot breathe, drowning under the heavy air. Now I live in the United States. I assumed that my new government would care, care about our dying planet, care about the People of Color disproportionately affected by climate change—but they did not and still don't.

Politicians have consistently ignored Indigenous Peoples and People of Color, those most affected by climate change. (These) communities experience higher rates of health-related illnesses caused by climate change, even though they contribute the least. Each day, vulnerable, underprivileged communities are plagued by drought, famine and respiratory problems. Each day, young people die because the United States and other governments have ignored the climate crisis for over 40 years. This is why so many young people today, especially youth of color, who are most impacted by climate change, are fighting. Unimpressed with political sound bites, and politicians ignoring climate justice for decades, young people everywhere are refusing to settle for anything less than transformational change.

As a member of Zero Hour, a youth-led movement that centers diverse voices in the fight for environmental justice, I, along with countless others, aim to take concrete action.

—Ahmad Ibsais

Ahmad Ibsais, *19, is a Palestinian American immigrant and activist fighting for human rights and against the climate crisis. A public health and political science student, he studies the intersection of healthcare equality in relation to climate, gun control and social justice.*

RACISM

THE DOCTRINE OF Discovery and its impacts are felt to this day by Indigenous Peoples around the world. The legacy is evident in the racism (the belief in the superiority of one race over the other) embedded in modern legal decisions, government land-use and resource-development priorities, deficiencies in (or lack of) healthcare and emergency response during disasters, and in many people's attitudes toward Indigenous Peoples and People of Color. One example is the ongoing attempt by the Bolivian government to remove Indigenous Peoples from the Amazon rainforest to allow deforestation projects to go ahead without protest. Another is the lower level of help given to People of Color during and following Hurricane Katrina in New Orleans.

The racist view that Indigenous Peoples, People of Color, poor people and other marginalized communities are inferior and don't matter continues to be used to "justify" the exploitation of their land and communities as *sacrifice zones* where polluting industrial plants, mines or pipelines are so often located. Indigenous and other marginalized people around the world have been fighting for their rights, their land and their lives for a long time.

> Indigenous and other marginalized people around the world have been fighting for their rights, their land and their lives for a long time.

91

INDUSTRIALIZATION

JAMES WATT'S IMPROVEMENT on the steam engine, which he introduced in 1776, and the use of coal as the energy source to run it, removed two major impediments to colonialism and industrialization: the intermittent nature of wind (for moving ships) and water (to power factories). Coal-powered steam engines ran at a consistent rate all the time and could be built anywhere, not just near water. They provided so much energy that they spurred the explosive growth in manufacturing during the Industrial Revolution. Oil, discovered in the mid-1800s, contained even more energy per unit than coal and could be more easily transported. Coal and oil led to a rapid increase in the standard of living for many people (although not for all). Coal and oil gave us electric lights, power tools, cars, cheap clothing and easy travel. Industrialists could move production to wherever resources were abundant and labor was cheapest. For the countries that industrialized early on, such as the United Kingdom, the United States, Canada, Australia, New Zealand and those in Europe, fossil fuels were wonderful discoveries.

But there's no free lunch in ecology. The waste products from extracting and burning fossil fuels pollute the air we breathe, the water we drink and the soil in which we grow our food. Digging up fossil fuels destroys the land and displaces people, communities and wildlife. These problems are relatively obvious (although that hasn't stopped us from producing and using fossil fuels), but what was not evident for a long time was the issue of greenhouse gas pollution and global heating. That's because greenhouse gases are invisible, they build up in the atmosphere, and it takes a long time for their impact to be noticed. We are good at pretending that what we can't see doesn't exist, but greenhouse gases don't recognize borders and spread out through the atmosphere everywhere, affecting everybody. We are only now starting to realize the full effects of our past and current ways of thinking and acting.

BURNING QUESTION

WHY DIDN'T WE ACT EARLIER?

BIG OIL KNEW! So did Big Coal! As far back as 1977, more than 10 years before the first public testimony about global warming by atmospheric scientist James Hansen, the fossil fuel industry's own scientists were presenting evidence that burning fossil fuels was causing climate change and warning that it would lead to catastrophic impacts early in the 21st century. At first the industry seemed to take the warnings seriously, advising reductions in fossil fuel combustion. Then, in 1989, several companies formed the Global Climate Coalition. Its purposes were to cast doubt on climate science and lobby against greenhouse gas reductions. Since then fossil fuel corporations have poured billions into misleading the public and buying the votes of elected officials to prevent restrictions on their activities. As a result, climate action has been delayed—at great cost to human society and the environment.

Sound like a crime against humanity? In *Unprecedented Crime: Climate Science Denial and Game Changers for Survival*, Peter D. Carter and Elizabeth Woodworth argue just that. They say those responsible for the cover-up should be charged and tried at the International Criminal Court. What do you think?

CAPITALISM

THE INDUSTRIAL REVOLUTION created the conditions for private ownership of the means of production for most of the things we use. Not everyone could own a factory or a fleet of ships. Industrialization also needed a mechanism for selling all those consumer goods it produced. Industrial capitalism emerged during the Industrial Revolution and is the dominant economic system in the world today. Capitalism concentrates the means of production in relatively few hands. This requires most of the rest of the population to exchange labor for wages. The products are sold for profit, and prices are determined by market competition. Capitalism relies on the money system, banking and credit, and thrives on externalizing costs.

The profit-driven market system has led to abundant material goods, but at its core it requires endless growth in the economy, which is at odds with a finite planet. Capitalism's main objective is to turn nature (trees, minerals, water, carbon, etc.) and people (labor) into consumer goods in order to make money for those few in charge of production and the financial system. The measure of the monetary value of all goods and services produced by a country over a certain period of time is known as the ***gross domestic product (GDP)***. The goal has been to keep the GDP going up year after year. The "side effects"—air and water pollution, ecological destruction, inequality, displacement, loss of life, changes in climate—aren't factored into the calculations.

Today 1 percent of the world's population owns half the wealth! In 2019, 26 of the wealthiest people had more wealth than 3.8 billion people. Capitalism has failed to benefit the world's majority. Most people on Earth are not wealthier, healthier or happier because of capitalism, but often the opposite.

RIGHTS FOR CORPORATIONS? WHAT ABOUT THE RIGHTS OF NATURE?

IN THE UNITED STATES, corporations have been granted some of the same constitutional rights as people, such as free speech and the right to give money to political candidates. This has expanded their political and economic influence on government, mostly to the detriment of the environment. What about the rights of nature? In 2008 Ecuador became the first country to give rights to nature under its constitution. The 2010 Universal Declaration of Rights of Mother Earth was created in Bolivia at a World People's Conference on Climate Change and the Rights of Mother Earth and has been signed by more than 800,000 people. The declaration accepts that Earth is a living being with inherent rights and outlines humankind's obligations to protect those rights.

Unfortunately, ecocide (destruction of nature) is legal pretty much everywhere. The Stop Ecocide campaign is working to amend international criminal law to make ecocide a crime against humanity. It would mean that the heads of the corporations doing the damage, and the government ministers who approve the permits allowing it, would be held criminally responsible for large-scale destructive activities and tried at the International Criminal Court. Supporters hope the amendment will prevent ecocide in the first place.

WHY GO TO SCHOOL WHEN I'M NOT SURE I HAVE A FUTURE?

IT MIGHT SEEM futile to go to school right now, but schools are pretty important places for developing young people's knowledge and attitudes. And many children around the world can't go to school and wish they could. Would you feel differently if your school focused on climate education and action? How does your school rate? Many of the high school students I interviewed told me they learned about climate change science in school but not about solutions, the underlying causes of the problem or issues of climate justice. School climate strikers are supported by their schools and teachers in some jurisdictions, but not in others. In some school districts, the fossil fuel industry even writes curriculum! As you can imagine, their message is not about kicking the fossil fuel habit or shutting down the industry.

Things are changing slowly. A Portland, Oregon, school district, through its 2016 Climate Justice Resolution, was one of the first to include activism and civic engagement in its official policy. Teachers are allowed to teach climate justice in the way they want to and support student activism against the fossil fuel industry and for real climate solutions. Schools for Climate Action, part of the National Children's Campaign in the United States, works to "empower schools to speak up for climate action."

In 2019 New Zealand created optional courses about the climate crisis for 11- to 15-year-olds. The curriculum, written by scientists and available to all schools in the country, includes information to help students plan their own activism and process eco-anxiety. In 2020 Italy became the first country to make it mandatory to teach students about climate change and sustainability. Mexico has also committed to increased environmental and climate change education in its schools.

NEOLIBERALISM

BY THE MID-1970S and '80s, governments in the United Kingdom and the United States realized that capitalism was creating social problems and tried to fix them by interfering in the market system. In reaction, an ideology called *neoliberalism* arose among political and economic thinkers. Neoliberalism's prime objective is to support corporations (aka the wealthy). It believes in tax cuts for corporations, deregulation of their operations, privatization of the commons (nature, education, healthcare, etc.), extreme regulation of the public sector, weaker collective bargaining for unions and support of *individualism*. Small government, large corporations.

Free-market neoliberalism has been embraced by industrialized countries and has allowed capitalism and corporations to spread their influence around the world through globalization, *free trade* agreements and militarization (the use of police and the military to secure access to resources). It has embedded corporate influence in all sectors of society, including the media, and has blurred the link between the fossil fuel industry and government. It has given corporations free rein to cut down forests for timber and agriculture, drain wetlands, overfish, dig up minerals, burn fossil fuels, poison water and air, and exploit and displace communities the world over, all in the name of progress, growth and profit.

Since 1988 the world has emitted more greenhouse gases than were emitted in the previous 100 years. For the reasons just mentioned, such as the perpetual-growth mentality and corporate influence on government decision making, neoliberalism and capitalism have made it harder for governments to do anything meaningful about the climate crisis. To make matters worse, the fossil fuel industry has known for decades what its products are doing to the planet and has spent (and continues to spend) billions of dollars to convince us of the opposite. It's clear we have neoliberalism and capitalism to thank for the climate and ecological crisis, right?

CONSUMERISM

Shop Stop, buying only necessities, is one of youth activist Greta Thunberg's solutions to the climate crisis.

NOT ENTIRELY. What about us, the people? We're the consumers who buy the products the corporations make. Household consumption contributes more than 60 percent of global greenhouse gas emissions and accounts for 50 to 80 percent of total land, material and water use. Much of the impact, about three-quarters, comes from the supply chain, from the extraction of raw materials right through to purchase. Pick something you bought recently. Your smartphone, for instance. Do you know what it's made of, how the raw materials were obtained, where and how it was made, how it got to the store? Each of those steps has an ecological footprint.

Maybe we've been duped by the fossil fuel industry into thinking everything is okay or duped into trusting that government is looking after things. But the reality is we're all complicit, particularly those of us who live consumer lifestyles. Since we're all in the same boat, pointing fingers isn't going to get us where we need to go, but rowing all together, and in the same direction, might.

EDUCATION IS A TOP CLIMATE SOLUTION

YOU MIGHT BE SURPRISED to hear that educating girls and women is a climate solution. Project Drawdown is a nonprofit organization that seeks to "help the world reach 'drawdown'—the future point in time when levels of greenhouse gases in the atmosphere stop climbing and start to steadily decline." The organization has analyzed hundreds of solutions and recommends many that, if implemented together, will stop global heating. Health and education—which includes both educating girls and family planning—is considered a top drawdown solution. Together, educating girls and family planning have the potential to reduce greenhouse gas emissions by over 85 gigatons of CO_2 (equivalents) by 2050. Studies show that the more years of schooling a woman has, the fewer children she has. The children are better fed, healthier and more likely to go to school themselves. Education is an effective and humanitarian way to reduce population (imagine the alternatives). Educated women and girls are more resilient to the shocks and disruptions from natural disasters and extreme weather brought on by global heating. They are often the stewards of the natural systems that support their families and the heart of their communities. Reducing barriers to education includes making schooling affordable, reducing the time and distance needed to attend (free bikes!), helping girls overcome health barriers (free healthcare) and making schools more friendly to girls (excellent teachers).

-4-

CHANGE-MAKERS AND CLIMATE HEROES

"Change will not come if we wait for some other person or some other time. We are the ones we've been waiting for. We are the change that we seek."

—BARACK OBAMA,
FORMER PRESIDENT OF THE UNITED STATES

– WE WERE BORN INTO A WORLD WITH AN EXPIRY DATE –

WHEN I WAS four years old, my dad's lungs stopped working because the air he was breathing was so polluted that it poisoned him. When I was seven years old, my mum was arrested and detained for trying to prevent trees from being cut down to make way for a shopping center. When I was 10 and 11 and 12, I heard about people starving, animals going extinct and natural resources being obliterated. Then when I was 15, I began to struggle to breathe on a daily basis because the panic and desperation I felt in the midst of all this was overwhelming.

What I've known throughout my life is that climate change is personal. It is the air we breathe, the food we eat and the money we spend. Climate change is the one thing that will not discriminate in its destruction of not only the human species, but of all living things. To claim that it is a distant threat and not consequential to individual action is to blatantly deny the truth and, in turn, incriminate oneself. It is no longer a case of economic or political background, of ethnicity or location, of age or gender, but of a want for survival and actively opposing all that challenges such.

—Talia Woodin

Talia Woodin, *22, was the media and messaging coordinator with the Extinction Rebellion Youth national team and now works as a freelance photographer and activist with various climate campaigns. She lives in London, UK.*

YOUR GENERATION IS leading the fight against the climate crisis. Perhaps you are among the millions of youth activists who have been striking from school and marching with Fridays For Future, demanding climate action from those who created the problems—world leaders, older generations and the fossil fuel industry. Perhaps you are suing your government for not protecting you and future generations. Perhaps you are using your personal talents and interests to add your voice in a creative way. As tomorrow's leaders, you have gained the *moral authority* to make demands. It might not feel like it sometimes, but you are being heard. Your generation is in the news, at the global climate meetings and in court. Even the climate skeptics are paying attention to you, although not always in the politest of language. I write this chapter as a celebration of your efforts.

I know from talking to many youth climate activists that you are also angry, tired and frightened. It's frustrating to work so hard for change and feel like nothing is happening. I write this chapter to let you know you are not alone. Many people, from many walks of life and from many organizations, have been working tirelessly for decades and continue to work to bring about positive change. Your generation stands on their shoulders. They continue to lift you up. You are carrying on their legacy. I know many of them are working alongside you. I don't have enough space in one short book to mention all the changemakers and climate heroes. Because this book has an international focus, I've mostly, with a few exceptions, included those who have a global presence. But I applaud all the national and local groups and individuals who are making a difference in their regions, where the most effective work can happen. In my mind, everyone who is contributing to the conversation is a climate hero.

BURNING QUESTION

WHAT CAREER SHOULD I CHOOSE?

PRETTY MUCH ANY career (except maybe CEO of a fossil fuel corporation!) can be directed toward a clean, green economy. Wind and solar technicians are among the fastest-growing (and well-paid) occupations. According to the US Bureau of Labor Statistics, for every fossil fuel job, you need several in solar to produce the equivalent amount of energy. Jobs in the caring and helping professions, such as nursing, teaching, counseling, home care, conflict management and social work, will be much needed. The age of regeneration will require restoration specialists, *agroecologists*, green engineers and clean-up specialists. We'll still rely on the knowledge and expertise of climate scientists and other kinds of specialists. We'll need skilled people in the trades to work in the *circular economy*, retrofitting buildings, repairing stuff and figuring out how to recycle better. Climate-aware urban planners, politicians who are not afraid to make the right decisions and community organizers are essential. What would life be without the creative arts? Pursue your passion, and there's no doubt you'll make the world a better place.

YOUTH

YOUTH FROM AROUND the world have mobilized to do what many adults have failed to do: protect the intergenerational right of children to a healthy, peaceful future. Youth of color, Indigenous youth, LGBTQ+ youth and other young people from all socioeconomic situations have been working to make change, some for decades. In 1992, 12-year-old Severn Cullis-Suzuki, representing the Environmental Children's Organization, gave a powerful speech at the Earth Summit in Rio de Janeiro, Brazil. She appealed to world leaders to stop the destruction of the environment, saying, "If you don't know how to fix it, please stop breaking it!" (You can hear the complete speech, recited by children, at severncullissuzuki.com.) Her words still resonate today. She didn't stop there though. In 2000 she cycled across Canada with five friends to raise awareness about the climate crisis and air pollution. She also started the Skyfish Project, a youth think tank which ran until 2004. Now married with two children, Severn continues to write and speak out as an environment and culture activist.

Earth Guardians started in 1992 as a school in Maui, Hawaii, where students were taught about environmental awareness and action. The students worked in their local community to restore sandalwood forests and stop the toxic burning of sugarcane. Their efforts gained attention, even from the Dalai Lama. In 1997, wanting to reach more people, the school moved to Colorado and continued its work of teaching youth about political action and activism. Today the organization has more than 300 Earth Guardian crews, in 60 countries. The youth crews use art, music, storytelling, on-the-ground projects, civic engagement and legal action to work

THIS IS ZERO HOUR IS A CHANGEMAKER!

The youth-led organization, with sister chapters across the globe, organizes climate marches and youth climate summits, advocates for climate justice and promotes the Green New Deal.

toward solving environmental, climate and social-justice problems. You can find out if there's a crew in your area by visiting the Earth Guardian website.

When she was 16, Colombian-born American Jamie Margolin became frustrated with the lack of political action on the climate crisis and how youth voices were being ignored in the conversation, even though young people would be the most affected. In 2017 she and her friends Nadia Nazar, Madeline Tew and Zanagee Artis started the Zero Hour climate action group to organize a mass youth-led day of protest. The first Zero Hour event took place over three days in July 2018 in Washington, DC, where more than 100 youth presented science-based demands for action on the climate crisis to federal elected officials. The next day they held a Youth Climate Art Festival, and on July 21, youth marched on the National Mall in Washington, DC, and in 25 sister marches around the world in the first Youth Climate March. You can read Zero Hour's guiding principles and join the movement at thisiszerohour.org.

I'm sure I don't need to tell you about Greta Thunberg, the young Swedish climate activist who started going on strike from school in 2018 to show politicians how worried she is about the climate crisis. She protested outside the Swedish parliament every Friday with a sign that read *Skolstrejk för klimatet* (School strike for climate). People started joining her, and she gained a lot of media attention. Her action inspired other high school students around the world to strike from school on Fridays, and the Fridays For Future movement was born. The momentum started by Greta and other youth-led organizations like Earth Guardians and Zero Hour culminated in the biggest international protest march in history in March 2019. Two million people joined in over 2,000 marches in 137 countries. In one week in November of that year, over seven million people (including my husband and me) walked out of work and school to demand climate action. Greta has continued to strike on Fridays even as she travels through Europe and North America by train, bus, sailboat and electric car to speak at international climate summits, national parliaments and youth climate marches, spreading her message to world leaders: Listen to the climate science and start taking action now! You can read her inspiring speeches in her book *No One Is Too Small to Make a Difference*.

Children don't normally sue governments, but some are taking this courageous route to force governments to act on the climate crisis. In 2015, 21 youth plaintiffs, supported by the nonprofit law firm Our Children's Trust, filed a constitutional climate lawsuit against the United States. Their complaint asserts that "through the government's affirmative actions that cause climate change, it has violated the youngest generation's constitutional rights to life, liberty and property, as well as failed to protect essential public trust resources." *Juliana v United States* is working its way through the long, convoluted legal process, with some wins and some losses.

YOU DRIVE, WORK, PAY TAXES.

#VOTE16

YOUR VOICE SHOULD COUNT.

Since it's you, the young people of today, who are going to be most impacted by the climate crisis in the future, shouldn't you be able to vote? With only a few exceptions (Austria and Malta), the voting age in most countries is 18 or older. Vote16 is a campaign to lower the voting age to 16 and to encourage young people to become politically engaged early.

People of all ages are supporting the lawsuit by holding rallies and submitting *amicus curiae* (friends of the court) briefs. Fifteen briefs from supportive communities were filed, including one organized by Earth Guardians and signed by 32,000 youth under the age of 25. The youngest plaintiff, Levi, then 12, wrote on the *Youth v Gov* website: "Every time I see the street flood outside my house, I think about how fragile our barrier island is. If sea level rise continues, that means the island I spent my whole entire life on will eventually go underwater."

In 2017, 15 young people from across Canada launched a lawsuit against their federal government. *La Rose et al. v. Her Majesty the Queen*, supported by the David Suzuki Foundation with assistance from Our Children's Trust, demands that the Canadian government

THE JULIANA PLAINTIFFS ARE CHANGEMAKERS!

Twenty-one American youth filed a constitutional climate
lawsuit against the US government in 2015.

"stop violating Charter rights by perpetuating dangerous climate change and develop an adequate, science-based climate plan now." Sophia, a plaintiff from Metepenagiag First Nation, a Mi'kmaq community in New Brunswick, sees the impact of the climate crisis on her community's ability to hunt, fish and gather traditional foods and to pass that cultural knowledge on to young people like herself. Our Children's Trust supports youth-led legal actions around the world.

Indigenous youth and youth of color are some of the strongest voices for climate action and climate justice. Here are a few of the many Indigenous youth activists fighting to protect their cultures and the environment.

INDIGENOUS YOUTH ACTIVISTS

XIUHTEZCATL MARTINEZ, an Aztec climate activist since the age of six and a hip hop artist, is one of the youth directors at Earth Guardians. He works tirelessly to inspire his generation to take action to protect the planet.

Singer-songwriter, actress and climate activist **TA'KAIYA BLANEY** from the Tla'amin First Nation in British Columbia has used her talents since age 10 to spread her message around the world. Check out her award-winning music video for "Earth Revolution," a song she co-wrote with Aileen De La Cruz.

INDIA LOGAN-RILEY from Te Ara Whatu, a group of young Maori and Pasifika activists in New Zealand, works to keep Indigenous Rights on the table at the highest decision-making levels, including at UN climate conferences.

HELENA GUALINGA from the Ecuadorian Amazon has been spreading the word about the impacts of the climate crisis on her region since she was a young child.

EMMANUELA SHINTA, a Dayak activist, filmmaker and writer from Indonesian Borneo, started the Ranu Welum Foundation to empower young Dayaks to document the island's destruction and stand up for their rights.

CHAITALI SHIVA GAVIT, a member of the Warli Tribe that lives in the Aarey Forest suburb of Mumbai, India, has been arrested for protesting the Mumbai government's decision to cut down thousands of trees in her tribe's homeland.

Environmental activist **BERTHA ZÚÑIGA CÁCERES** of the Lenca people of Honduras is carrying on the legacy of her mother, Berta Cáceres, who was assassinated in 2016 for her work fighting to bring social and environmental justice to the Indigenous Peoples of her country. Bertha is the general coordinator of the Civic Council of Popular and Indigenous Organizations of Honduras, which defends Indigenous communities from mining, dam construction and logging.

ARTEMISA XAKRIABÁ, an Indigenous climate activist from São João das Missões in Brazil, is a youth leader in the movement to stop environmental destruction across Brazil—especially in the Amazon rainforest.

In 2016, protesters in Toronto marched in solidarity with the Standing Rock Indigenous Uprising to stop the Dakota Access Pipeline.

The International Indigenous Youth Council (IIYC) was formed during the Standing Rock Indigenous Uprising of 2016 to protect the Cannonball and Missouri Rivers from the construction of the Dakota Access Pipeline. The youth-led organization now has chapters across North America (referred to by Indigenous Peoples as Turtle Island), all working to organize and inspire Indigenous youth through education, spiritual practices and civic engagement to become leaders working for social justice and the protection of water, land and treaty rights. IIYC collaborated with other youth-led groups, including Zero Hour, Fridays For Future, Extinction Rebellion Youth and Earth Guardians, to organize the 50th-anniversary Earth Day 2020 march, held virtually with livestreaming music, speakers, at-home activities and an online strike through social media because of the global COVID-19 pandemic.

INDIGENOUS-LED ORGANIZATIONS

NDIGENOUS YOUTH CLIMATE activists are among the many Indigenous Peoples around the world who have been defending their rights and their traditional lands since European contact. As stewards of almost 45 percent of the planet, Indigenous Peoples are often on the front lines, protesting both extractivism and climate issues and leading the resistance against fossil fuel projects and government policies and decisions that threaten their way of life, their sacred places and their cultures.

In April 2009, Indigenous representatives from around the world, including the Arctic, North America, Asia, the Pacific region, Latin America, Africa, the Caribbean and Russia, met in Anchorage, Alaska, for the first Indigenous Peoples' Global Summit on Climate Change. The result was the Anchorage Declaration, a unified statement upholding Indigenous Rights through the United Nations

In January 2020, 60 peasant youth from Thailand, South Korea, Indonesia, Philippines, Nepal, India, Pakistan, Bangladesh and Sri Lanka met in Sri Lanka for the first Asian Continental Youth Assembly of La Via Campesina. The youth of La Via Campesina work for agrarian reform and food sovereignty and recognize agroecology as key to tackling the climate crisis.

Declaration on the Rights of Indigenous Peoples (UNDRIP)—more on UNDRIP in chapter 5—and calling on world leaders to take climate action in a way that respects Indigenous Rights and includes Indigenous Peoples.

The Indigenous Environmental Network (IEN) is an "alliance of Indigenous Peoples whose mission is to protect the sacredness of Earth Mother from contamination and exploitation by strengthening, maintaining and respecting Indigenous teachings and natural laws." IEN programs are focused primarily in North America, often in collaboration with other grassroots organizations to further their common goals.

La Via Campesina is an international peasants' movement involving 182 organizations that represent 200 million small-scale and rural farmers, many of them Indigenous, in 81 countries. The organization fights *for* food sovereignty, climate and environmental justice, dignity for migrant and wage workers, and land, water and territorial rights for its members. It fights *against* transnational companies and agribusiness, patriarchy, capitalism and so-called free trade.

ENVIRONMENTALISTS

MANY LONG-TIME ENVIRONMENTAL groups, such as Greenpeace, the Sierra Club and the World Wildlife Fund, actively campaign for climate action, but I have focused on a few of the grassroots organizations that are concerned entirely with the climate crisis and invite active participation by the public. In his book *Oil and Honey: The Education of an Unlikely Activist*, Bill McKibben tells the story of how he and a few of his students at Middlebury College in Vermont gave birth in 2008 to what has become 350.org, one of the most well-known grassroots environmental organizations focused on the climate crisis. You've probably guessed already that the 350 stands for 350 ppm. The group's website calls 350.org an "international movement of ordinary people." Its goals are a rapid and just transition to 100 percent renewable energy, using community-led solutions, no new fossil fuel projects and "not a penny more for dirty energy." 350.org was instrumental in organizing the first global days of action, including the International Day of Climate Action in 2009, the Global Work Party in 2010 and Moving Planet in 2011. The organization also started the fossil fuel–***divestment*** movement, which is discussed in the next chapter. If you want to organize climate actions, 350.org is a good place to go for help. Bill McKibben is a funny, easy-going type, but he's really serious about his climate work. He's been arrested for civil disobedience several times. Bill has written many articles and books about the climate crisis, including *The End of Nature* and *Falter: Has the Human Game Begun to Play Itself Out?*

Another unlikely but famous activist is former US vice president Al Gore. You may have seen his film *An Inconvenient Truth*. In 2009 he started the Climate Reality Project to empower "everyday people to become activists." The project trains people of all ages to become Climate Reality leaders, who go out into their communities to inspire action on climate solutions. As of 2020, the Climate Reality leadership core had trained more than 20,000 leaders in over 150 countries.

Extinction Rebellion (XR) describes itself as an "international [do-it-together] movement that uses nonviolent civil resistance in an attempt to halt mass extinction and minimize the risk of social collapse." XR members believe that the only way to bring about the needed radical systems change is to disrupt the status quo, and they do it in lots of creative ways. XR started in 2018 in London, England, when more than 1,500 people

350.ORG IS A CHANGEMAKER!

Started by American professor Bill McKibben and his students, 350.org inspires people around the world. Hundreds of people in Mexico City formed this Living 350.org Sun to raise awareness about alternative energy as a solution to climate change.

gathered to deliver a Declaration of Rebellion to the UK government. Since then dozens of XR groups have started up around the world, including Extinction Rebellion Youth, which is for anyone born after 1990 and has over 127 youth groups internationally.

I named my electric car NK after one of my climate heroes, the writer and activist Naomi Klein. Naomi co-authored the Leap Manifesto, a document that outlines how "Canada can move to a clean-energy economy in a way that addresses systemic racism and economic inequality." It led to the formation of The Leap, an environmental organization dedicated to "advancing systemic change in the face of our intersecting crises of climate change, inequality, and racism." While it has been operating mostly in Canada and the United States, the organization has inspired the Scandinavian Green Manifesto, as well as sister Leap initiatives in Australia and the United Kingdom.

CIVIL RESISTANCE

SOME PEOPLE CHOOSE to get arrested as a form of climate activism. Peaceful civil resistance (also known as civil disobedience) is a long-standing and proven way to change society for the better. Challenging unjust laws through strikes, boycotts, blockades, mass protests and other nonviolent means was instrumental in the success of Gandhi's Salt March against British rule in India, the Black civil-rights movement in the United States and, in many countries, the women's suffrage movement to gain the vote. Civil resistance aims to disrupt the status quo in a way that has an economic cost to the people running the world. It puts governments in a dilemma that opens an opportunity for things to change. Nonviolent disruption has succeeded more often than violent disruption, which often leads to fascism and authoritarianism. One young activist I interviewed commented that other youth climate activists from countries with authoritarian governments seemed less comfortable with the idea of civil disobedience because their human rights were more likely to be abused by their government.

Poet, teacher and Water & Land Defender Rita Wong was arrested in 2018 and sentenced to 28 days in prison for blockading the construction of the TransMountain tar sands oil pipeline in Burnaby, BC. At her sentencing hearing she stated, "We can all learn from natural law and Coast Salish law that we have a reciprocal relationship with the land; and that we all have a responsibility to care for the land's health, which is ultimately our health too."

A group of scientists in Germany, Switzerland and Austria started Scientists for Future in 2019 in support of the Fridays For Future youth movement.

SCIENTISTS

S CIENTISTS ARE NOT often known for their political activism. They are taught to be objective, to be critical of their own research and to avoid expressing their personal opinions. In November 2019 a document prepared by the Alliance of World Scientists was published in the journal *BioScience*, declaring that "planet Earth is facing a climate emergency." The declaration was signed by 11,258 scientists (including me) from 153 countries. The fact that so many scientists are mobilizing to speak forcefully to world leaders indicates how serious the climate crisis is. Some scientists are even willing to get arrested to make their point. Over 1,500 scientists have written another declaration called "Scientists' Declaration of Support for Non-Violent Direct Action against Government Inaction over the Climate and Ecological Emergency." There's even a Scientists for Extinction Rebellion Facebook page.

Marine biologist Rachel Carson is famous for her 1962 book *Silent Spring*, in which she warned the world about the harm of pesticides to wildlife populations and humans. Her writings are credited with starting the modern environmental movement. She died of breast cancer in 1964 at age 56, but her message of environmental awareness lives on today.

James Hansen was the head of the World Meteorological Association when he was asked to speak to the United States Senate in 1988 about current scientific knowledge of the changing climate. When the shy atmospheric scientist reported that global warming was real and humans were responsible, the Senate altered his published testimony. That made him mad, and he embarked on a long and winding path to climate activism. He's been arrested many times for civil disobedience, has written numerous books, articles and opinion pieces about climate science, speaks publicly on the subject and is involved with the Our Children's Trust youth climate lawsuit *Juliana v United States*. His granddaughter Sophie is one of the child plaintiffs. Hansen currently heads the Climate Science, Awareness and Solutions lab at Columbia University, where he continues his research.

Michael E. Mann is an atmospheric scientist and geophysicist at Penn State University, director of the Earth System Science Center and a contributor to the Intergovernmental Panel on Climate Change (IPCC) reports. When he published the now famous "hockey stick graph" that showed the sharp upward climb of temperature in response to anthropogenic greenhouse gas emissions, he was relentlessly attacked in the media by climate change deniers. The experience turned him into a public figure. He's written four books, including *The Hockey Stick and the Climate Wars: Dispatches from the Front Lines*. He co-founded the climate science website *Real Science* (realscience.org), which publishes "climate science by working climate scientists for the interested public and journalists."

Indian physicist and social activist Vandana Shiva has dedicated her life to the most significant ecological and social issues of our times, including the climate crisis, and works closely with local communities and social movements in many areas of sustainability, most notably in the area of agriculture and food. She has written many books critical of world leaders and industry and isn't afraid to speak her mind. She's justly considered an environmental hero.

VANDANA SHIVA IS A CLIMATE HERO!

One of her many accomplishments is the founding of Navdanya (nine seeds), a women-centered movement of seedkeepers and organic producers in India. Its goal is the protection of cultural and biological diversity.

Katharine Hayhoe is one of my favorite climate heroes because she has a talent for explaining climate science and what it means to all of us in clear, understandable, positive language. Check out her Global Weirding videos and her TED talk. She's also a brilliant climate scientist working at the top of her field. She's currently a professor in the Department of Political Science and a director of the Climate Center at Texas Tech University. I honestly don't know how she finds the time to do research, write papers and key government reports, lead climate-impact assessments, give public talks, write books, make films and still hang out with her husband (and stay so cheerful).

I can't leave out biologist Jane Goodall, famous for her work with chimpanzees, whose Roots & Shoots program trains and inspires youth to become community environmental leaders. Or David Suzuki (father of Severn), who went from being a geneticist in a lab to a world-renowned environmental activist, television and radio personality, writer and founder of the David Suzuki Foundation.

JANE GOODALL IS A CLIMATE HERO!

Her Roots & Shoots program inspires youth to "make positive change in their communities."

POLITICAL LEADERS

WHILE SOME POLITICAL leaders continue to deny the climate crisis as their countries burn, or argue about details as greenhouse gas emissions escalate, not all world leaders, politicians and bureaucrats are climate slackers. In fact, most of them have been working hard on the world stage and in their own countries to bring about action on the climate crisis.

The same year (1988) that James Hansen told the US Senate human-caused global warming had begun, the World Meteorological Organization and the United Nations Environment Program established the IPCC to provide ongoing scientific assessments to guide international climate negotiations. The IPCC issued its first assessment in 1990, which led to the adoption of the United Nations Framework Convention on Climate Change (UNFCCC) in 1992. The treaty was opened for signing at the Earth Summit in Rio de Janeiro that year—the same year Severn Cullis-Suzuki gave her famous speech. The purpose of the convention was to "bring the world together to curb greenhouse gas emissions and adapt to climate change." The UNFCCC came into force in 1994, with nearly every country, referred to as the parties (197), signing on. The parties meet every year at the Conference of the Parties (COP) to further negotiations.

COP meetings are a big deal, attended by thousands of people from government, industry and environmental organizations. To date there have been 26 COPs, the most recent in Glasgow in November 2021. Major milestones include the 1997 adoption of the Kyoto Protocol, the first international treaty to reduce greenhouse gas emissions; the signing of the Copenhagen Accord, whereby developed countries pledged to spend US$30 billion over two years to help developing countries make the needed transition; and the adoption of the Paris Agreement in 2015 by 195 nations, with the goal of keeping the global temperature increase below 2 °C (3.6 °F) from pre-industrial times while aiming for 1.5 °C (2.7 °F). Each country has set its own voluntary nationally determined contribution (NDC) for meeting that goal and, presumably, is working toward it. Currently the sum of the targets isn't enough to stay below 2 °C, but each contribution is reviewed regularly and ratcheted up as needed. Risa Smith, who attended the 2019 COP on behalf of the International Union for Conservation of Nature, told me that some signatories of the Paris Agreement are increasing their efforts—a hopeful sign.

AREN'T ANY COUNTRIES STEPPING UP?

WHEN I LAST CHECKED climateactiontracker.org in August 2021, of the 36 countries analyzed, the tiny West African countries of the Gambia and Morocco were the only signatories to the Paris Agreement whose voluntary nationally determined contributions (NDCs) are compatible with global heating of under 1.5 °C (2.7 °F). That means if all governments adopted and met the same targets as these two countries, global heating would stay below 1.5 °C. The Gambia intends to meet its targets by investing in renewable energy; restoring forests, mangroves and savannas; replacing flooded rice paddies with dry upland rice fields; and promoting efficient cookstoves. Both countries will need international financial and technical support to succeed. Will somebody please give them a hand?

The NDCs of Bhutan, Costa Rica, Ethiopia, India, Kenya and Philippines were consistent with global heating under 2 °C (3.6 °F). The NDCs of all other signatories would result in increases above 2 °C. In 2021 the United States rejoined the Paris Agreement and submitted a more ambitious NDC. While this is good news, its target falls short of achieving the Paris Agreement's 1.5 °C limit.

She worries, though, that it won't be enough or in time. Targets must be supported by ambitious policies and actions. As of May 2021, all adopted national policies are projected to result in a temperature increase of 2.9 °C (5.2 °F) by 2100.

As you can tell, international negotiations are slow-moving and involve a lot of players, who don't always agree on how to get things done. The Climate Emergency Movement is attempting to speed things up. Its goal is for national, regional and local governments "to declare a climate emergency and mobilize society-wide resources at sufficient scale and speed to protect civilization, the economy, people, species and ecosystems." As of July 2021, climate emergencies had been declared by over 1900 local governments in 34 countries. Wales, Scotland, Ireland, Northern Ireland, the United Kingdom, Canada, the European Union, Portugal, France, Spain, Austria, Italy, Malta, Japan, South Korea, Bangladesh and Argentina are among the countries that have declared national climate emergencies. Declaring an emergency isn't sufficient, though. Declarations need to be backed by action, money and legislation.

Some elected officials are speaking out in creative ways. The entire parliament of the country of the Maldives donned scuba gear and held a cabinet meeting underwater to bring attention to the threat of sea level rise to their small island nation. Alexandria Ocasio-Cortez, often referred to as AOC, is the youngest woman to be elected to the US Congress. She's championing a Green New Deal, a resolution to transition the entire country to renewable energy and to reach net-zero greenhouse gas emissions by 2030. The Green New Deal in the United States is supported by the youth-led Sunrise Movement.

ARTISTS

MANY PEOPLE EXPRESS themselves through the creative arts. Writing is my way of speaking out, as it is for many authors who have published climate-related books. There are too many to list, but I've included quite a few in the Resources section of this book and in the complete references list on the Orca Book Publishers webpage for *Urgent Message*.

Josh Fox, director of *Gasland*, *Gasland Part II* and *How to Let Go of the World and Love All the Things Climate Can't Change*, makes films to protest hydraulic fracturing, or fracking, and horizontal drilling for natural gas in the United States.

Artist and architect Naziha Mestaoui created an artwork called *1 Heart 1 Tree* that invited citizens around the globe to turn the Eiffel Tower into a virtual forest. Each participant used an app with a heartbeat sensor to generate a virtual tree that "grew" to their own heartbeat. For every virtual tree created, a real tree was planted as part of one of seven global reforestation projects around the world.

Canadian activist, artist, author and songwriter Franke James posts climate-focused graphic essays on her website and created an award-winning music video for her song "Gasoline, Gasoline (The World's Aflame)."

Daniel Crawford, a geography student at the University of Minnesota, composed a song for string quartet, called "Planetary Bands, Warming World," that traces 135 years of rising average global temperature.

IT'S A JOURNEY

B.Y.O reusables

say no to supermarkets

make a compost toilet

grow something
Herbs   Salad

only buy 2nd hand

read all the things

local holidays

save seeds

get water tanks / solar

flight free

eat less meat

Protest

boycott fast fashion

eat 95% locavore
COMMUNITY GARDEN

Go plastic free

Divest

drive less

use your greywater

go car free

get outside more

go vegan/ ethical omnivore

fly less

right livelihood

grow most of your food

go chemical free
SOAP
make your own

Invest

use less plastic

compost
build soil

BRENNA QUINLAN IS A CHANGEMAKER!

Brenna is an illustrator and *permaculture* educator who uses her art and actions to make the world a better place. Along with creating message-packed climate-action illustrations, she teaches permaculture and is part of the Formidable Vegetable teaching team for the School Permaculture Tour. Brenna truly practices what she preaches. She lives a low-impact regenerative lifestyle in a passive solar tiny house at the permaculture demonstration community Melliodora in Central Victoria, Australia. You can see more of her amazing illustrations at brennaquinlan.com/art-as-activism.

PRIVATE CITIZENS

EVERYONE MENTIONED IN this chapter so far is a citizen of somewhere, but a few individuals really go out of their way to take a stand on the climate crisis.

For example, in 2008 university student Tim DeChristopher disrupted an auction for drilling rights in Utah by outbidding oil and gas companies for parcels around Arches and Canyonlands National Parks. Problem was, he didn't have the money to pay for them. He was convicted of fraud for his creative civil disobedience and spent 21 months in prison. Since then, he's helped organize Peaceful Uprising, a volunteer climate action group, and founded the Climate Disobedience Center, which supports climate dissidents.

In solidarity with Extinction Rebellion, Ann Cognito, a Canadian woman in her 50s, and her dog, Mr. Myrtle, traveled about 3,300 kilometers (2,050 miles) by kickbike, from Calgary to Ottawa, to deliver a letter demanding that the government tell the truth about the climate crisis and take drastic action to reduce greenhouse gas emissions to net zero by 2025.

These activists at the 2017 March for Science in Washington, DC, are undeterred by a little rain. We Exist Collective is a social movement that works to create accommodating and accessible spaces for activists with disabilities and to amplify their voices.

BURNING QUESTION

DO I NEED TO BECOME A VEGAN?

WHAT YOU EAT is a matter of personal choice. Some people become vegans because they feel strongly about the rights of animals. The production of red meat and dairy most certainly has a large footprint compared to plant based alternatives— bigger than the emissions from cars, planes, buses and boats combined. But switching to a 100 percent vegan or vegetarian diet to reduce your carbon footprint isn't necessary. In its 2018 special report *Global Warming of 1.5 °C*, the ipcc recommends eating less (not no) red meat and dairy in order to reduce greenhouse gas emissions from forest clearing for agriculture and from methane burped up by ruminants (cattle, sheep and goats).

Choosing to reduce your consumption of meat (especially beef and lamb) by 50 percent or more per week will make a huge difference. Add some new plant-based foods to your diet to take its place. Even replacing red meat with dairy is helpful. Grass-fed meat is better than grain-fed. Keep in mind that animals are an integral part of regenerative farming, and meat is an important component of health, food and economic security for many people around the world. I like the mantra of Michael Pollan, author of *In Defence of Food: An Eater's Manifesto*: "Eat food. Not too much. Mostly plants."

One of the wackiest climate actions I've come across is the World Naked Bike Ride. The clothing-optional event to protest oil dependency and car culture takes place in 20 countries and 70 cities every year. Each cyclist is going out of their way to reveal the bare facts.

Climate resistance can be as quiet and personal as your food choices (see reducetarian.org), what you wear (check out trashisfortossers.com) or what you do with old items (upcyclethat.com). Are you a knitter or someone who enjoys crafts? Sarah Corbett started the Craftivist Collective to encourage others, in the famous words of Mahatma Gandhi, to "be the change they want to see in the world" by making beautiful crafts. The collective has thousands of members who get together for stitch-ins. She's written a book called *How to Be a Craftivist: The Art of Gentle Protest.*

Not everyone is cut out for civil disobedience, marching (or cycling naked) in the streets or community organizing. The message is to use your passions, skills and talents to add your voice in the way in which you are most comfortable. The possibilities are limited only by your imagination. But what do all these young people, scientists, environmentalists, politicians, artists and citizens want? You can hear them in the streets shouting (or whispering as they knit), "Climate action!" When do they want it? "Now!"

Craftivist Jessica Liu started the Sewciety Project so that she and other teens could use their creative talents with a sewing machine to speak out about the climate crisis.

SCHOOL STRIKE
FOR
CLIMATE
#FridaysForFuture

- WITNESS -

I'M WITNESSING #CLIMATECHANGE. Half of my country is running out of water. We are experiencing a large drought. This summer we have had high temperatures, like never seen before. This is not a crazy scientific theory. This is reality.

—Nyombi Morris

Nyombi Morris, *23, is a climate activist from Uganda. His six-year-old sister, Kimberlyn, likes to join her big brother on climate strikes.*

-5-

WHAT NOW?

Solutions to the Climate Crisis

"If we strove to heal and protect every estuary, every forest, every wetland, every piece of damaged and desertified land, every coral reef, every lake, and every mountain, not only would most drilling, fracking, and pipelining have to stop, but the biosphere would become far more resilient too."

—CHARLES EISENSTEIN,
AUTHOR OF *CLIMATE: A NEW STORY*

WHEN I WROTE the proposal for this book, I planned to have a chapter about imagining the world we want to create. Then I started the research and learned that the world we want to create is already here! Individuals, communities, cities, whole countries are becoming cleaner, greener and more equitable. In the following pages you will learn about solutions to the climate crisis that already exist and that we need more of.

Everyone needs to step up to make it work, not just the big emitters. Forty percent of all emissions come from 170 countries, each of which emits less than 2 percent of annual global emissions. So even if the major emitters go to zero emissions, it won't be enough. We're all in this together. Everything we do has a consequence. Our choices will lead to a hotter planet or a cooler one. The choices we make today will determine our future.

We've done it before. In 1985 world leaders cooperated to create the Vienna Convention for the Protection of the Ozone Layer. Its purpose was to regulate an ozone-destroying class of greenhouse gases called chlorofluorocarbons (CFCs), which had caused a thinning of the ozone layer in the upper atmosphere, which protects us from the damaging effects of ultraviolet (UV) radiation. In 1989 the Montreal Protocol on Substances that Deplete the Ozone Layer came into effect, and within three decades the thinning had virtually stopped, with CFC levels in the atmosphere expected to return to 1989 levels by 2050. This global effort had another benefit. Without it, CFC greenhouse gases would have warmed the planet by an additional 1 °C (1.8 °F). In the same way, the COVID-19 pandemic proved to us that the world could come together and mobilize action and resources quickly to deal with a common threat. We've shown ourselves that if there's a will, there's a way.

- SUNRISE MOVEMENT -

THE SUNRISE MOVEMENT in the United States was started by Varshini Prakash in 2017 to build an "army of young people" to support a Green New Deal that will fight climate change and create millions of green jobs. With Sunrise hubs all over the country, the movement is a force to be reckoned with. Sunrisers aren't afraid to get arrested for what they believe in. During the COVID-19 pandemic, they created the Sunrise School, where youth connected online to build relationships with other young people, learn about the climate crisis and take action in creative ways.

It's clear we need to do much more than stop using fossil fuels and switch to renewable energy. We need to stop emitting greenhouse gases *and* remove carbon dioxide from the atmosphere. Then, to make the transition work, we need to transform the economic and political systems that created the problems to systems that are Earth- and community-centered and equitable for all, where everyone is treated fairly and past injustices are remedied. Without that shift we'll be sure to find ourselves in the same unhappy position as we're in today. Here's what I learned we need to do. All are equally important and are interconnected:

Stop burning fossil fuels.

Stop destroying nature and help it recover.

Transition to clean renewable energy.

Consume less.

Unite with and learn from Indigenous Peoples.

Do no harm (or as little as possible).

STOP BURNING FOSSIL FUELS

N THE DAVID SUZUKI FOUNDATION'S report *Zeroing in on Emissions: Canada's Clean Power Pathways*, writer Tom Green described the atmosphere as a bathtub. I like that analogy. We've all been pouring water (greenhouse gases) into the bathtub (atmosphere), but some of us have been adding more than others. To make matters worse, we've damaged the bathtub (by destroying nature) so it can't hold as much water as it used to. We know from current climate impacts that we've already overshot the safe level of 1 °C (1.8 °F) and 350 ppm. Our bathtub is overflowing and damaging our house. Ask the people in Australia, battling drought and bushfires; or the residents of Shishmaref in Alaska, who have to move their community because of sea level rise, permafrost melt and bigger storms; or citizens of Chennai, India, who are running out of water, if they want greenhouse gas emissions and the global average temperature to keep climbing.

How do we get it back to that safe level? First, we need to stop adding more water to the bathtub. We need to stop greenhouse gases at their source: the extraction and burning of fossil fuels. Each country needs to reduce its greenhouse gas emissions to net zero (the amount emitted equals the amount removed from the atmosphere). The more we reduce and the faster we do it, the better off we'll be. To do it fairly, the countries that industrialized first and are responsible for most of the emissions that have accumulated in the atmosphere so far—the United States, the United Kingdom, Germany, Canada and Russia—will need to cut their emissions the most and the fastest. How fast? As fast as possible.

Iva Jericevic traveled from Scotland to Serbia flight-free! A round-trip flight between London and New York causes about 3 m² (32 ft²) of Arctic sea ice to melt. Air travel accounts for 2.5 percent of annual global emissions, which seems like a small amount, but it benefits a relatively small proportion of the world's population (most can't afford it) and is expected to increase to as high as 15 percent by 2050. You can pledge to fly less at pledgetoflyless.co.uk or flightfree.co.uk.

The big emitters also need to help those developing countries with large and growing populations, like India and China, which have the potential to greatly increase their greenhouse gas emissions as they improve the standard of living for their citizens, build a clean-energy economy in order to avoid future emissions. Fossil fuels currently produce about 80 percent of the world's energy. How do we kick such an enormous addiction?

It's interesting to note that the restrictions on travel and other personal freedoms imposed during the COVID-19 pandemic reduced fossil fuel consumption dramatically. As lockdown restrictions were eased in the middle of 2020 in many countries, and some economic activities restarted, emissions began to increase again. Many people are advocating for a "green" COVID-19 economic recovery that focuses on emissions reductions.

STOP SUBSIDIZING FOSSIL FUELS

GOVERNMENTS MUST STOP SUBSIDIZING the fossil fuel industry. Fossil fuel subsidies are government actions that give fossil fuels an advantage over other energy sources. Subsidies are such things as direct payments, tax breaks, low-interest loans, or free land, water and electricity. According to one estimate, government subsidies to fossil fuel companies worldwide add up to at least $775 billion to $1 trillion every year. If one adds to this the costs of fossil fuels related to the climate crisis, environmental and health impacts, and military conflicts and spending, the total cost is upward of $6 trillion a year. That's about $10 million per minute!

Removing subsidies would make oil, coal and gas extraction and development less profitable for fossil fuel companies, so they would be more likely to leave the fossil fuels in the ground and retire existing projects. According to the Global Oil and Gas Network, emissions from currently operating oil and gas fields and mines will push global temperature rise beyond 1.5 °C (2.7 °F) by 2030. Current government-supported plans to produce fossil fuels are 120 percent more than the level of production needed to keep heating under 1.5 °C, let alone get back to the safe 1 °C (1.8 °F). It's clear that the fossil fuel industry is incompatible with a healthy planet and that most of the proven oil, coal and gas reserves must remain unburned or in the ground. Governments also need to phase out coal- and diesel-fired electricity production, tax methane emissions from natural-gas production and require fossil fuel companies to clean up after themselves.

So far, fossil fuel companies and most governments aren't voluntarily stepping up to end the production and burning of fossil fuels. Organizations and individuals have started pressuring them to do it by encouraging divestment from the fossil fuel industry. The same principles apply: cut the funding to fossil fuel producers and make them less profitable. Since 2014, Fossil Free (gofossilfree.org), a global fossil fuel–divestment movement started by 350.org, convinced more than 1200 institutions and 58,000 individuals to divest over $14 trillion in fossil fuel investment holdings.

Big banks invest trillions of dollars in fossil fuel projects. Every year since 2010 the Rainforest Action Network has published *Banking on Climate Change: Fossil Fuel Report Card*, which ranks the major banks' level of investment in the fossil fuel industry. While the financing of the fossil fuel industry continues to rise, things may be starting to change. In 2019 the European Investment Bank, the largest international public bank, announced it would stop lending money to most (but not all) fossil fuel projects. This follows Ireland's move to become the first country to pass a bill to completely divest from fossil fuels, although investments have continued. The Lofoten Declaration, a global initiative signed by over 500 organizations from 76 countries, asks for a managed decline of fossil fuel production, a reasonable request that so far has gone unheeded.

Cut the funding to fossil fuel producers and make them less profitable.

PUT A PRICE ON CARBON AND REGULATE IT

ECONOMISTS WILLIAM NORDHAUS AND PAUL ROMER won the 2018 Nobel Memorial Prize in economic sciences for showing that putting a price on carbon is the most effective way to lower greenhouse gas emissions. Their theory is that higher prices will encourage businesses and consumers to find alternatives to fossil fuels. It's also a way to account for the external costs of fossil fuels, such as repairing environmental degradation or funding healthcare. The pricing is in the form of a **carbon tax** (**carbon fee**) or through what's called **cap and trade**. In a cap-and-trade system, a government sets an upper limit (quota) on the amount of carbon a company or industry can emit, then allows emitters to exceed their quota by trading for unused quota from low emitters. Carbon fees are generally considered more efficient and less likely than cap and trade to be used as an excuse to pollute.

Globally, as of 2021, 64 carbon-pricing initiatives have been implemented. In the province of British Columbia, where I live, we've had a carbon tax on home heating, transportation and electricity (which covers about 70 percent of the province's emissions) since 2008. The tax is revenue neutral, which means it is returned to the consumer either through lowered personal and business income taxes or through a dividend check. It appears to be working. Between 2007 and 2016, emissions in British Columbia declined by 3.7 percent, even though the province's GDP rose by 19 percent. The tax is designed to increase over time to encourage greater reductions in greenhouse gases. In 2021, the BC carbon tax is scheduled to increase to $50/gigaton of carbon dioxide equivalents (includes the warming equivalent of methane and nitrous oxide). Some feel the tax needs to be much higher to speed up the necessary behavior changes.

In addition to imposing a carbon tax, governments can restrict greenhouse gas emissions by industry—for example, requiring fossil fuel companies to reduce or eliminate methane leaks during production and transportation of natural gas, or requiring airlines or shipping companies to use cleaner-burning fuels. The European Union is planning a carbon border tax on imported goods according to their carbon footprint.

- SURREAL -

BEFORE 2018, THINGS seemed to make sense. Global governance seemed reasonable, and the way I saw the world was smooth and beautiful. Everything was full of feeling.

Australia's first school strike in 2018 threw everything into sharp focus. Climate change, mentioned offhandedly, was something I'd mentally avoided confronting. It was a petition in my email that alerted me to the strike; it intellectually humbled me, gave me energy and started a downward spiral.

The smoother flow of childhood ended and I had an obligation to the world instead; I wrote, I thought, I entered a space—"activist"—that didn't feel right to me. Even now, a year on, it still doesn't feel like I've breathed.

My writing at the beginning was full of emotion; the direction of our world was like a high tragedy—I oscillated between acceptance of suffering and anger. I used one word a lot—*surreal*—and it still hits home.

I've swapped out childhood fantasy for tunnel-vision focus. I can comprehend more now, and I'm more self-aware; it feels like I have a greater confidence all through my body. But this situation is still so strange and sad, still so anxiety-inducing, full of dissociation. Following obligation is good—boy oh boy, I'm not "passionate" about climate change—but what I'm slowly learning is this: I need that time to breathe. Fight and flow can coexist.

—Veronica Hester

Veronica Hester, *17, is from Sydney, Australia, and enjoys science, debating and reading. Since 2018 she's been involved in a whirlwind of climate activism.*

Canadian teen climate activists Uma Le Daca (left) and Nina Rossing stepped out of their comfort zone and gave a presentation about climate justice and intersectionality to their elected officials at Vancouver City Hall.

WHAT CAN YOU DO?

SPEAK UP! MANY PEOPLE and organizations are urging governments and corporations to act. The online petition at StopFundingFossils.org demands an end to subsidies for oil, gas and coal companies. In addition to signing petitions, write a letter to your elected representative or, even better, organize a face-to-face meeting.

You may not have holdings to divest from yet, but your parents may. Try talking to them about their investments. As a parent, I know I want to do the right thing for my children. Do you have a bank account or a credit card? I recently switched my credit card from a big bank high on the *Banking on Climate Change* list to a credit union with good environmental policies. Tell your bank why you are switching.

Many people grumble about higher prices and government regulations, but the climate crisis will cost us much more in the future if we don't take action. You can help by accepting carbon fees and regulations designed to lower greenhouse gas emissions. Encourage your friends and family to do the same, and if there aren't any fees and regulations where you live, ask your elected representatives to bring them in.

STOP DESTROYING NATURE AND HELP IT RECOVER

SINCE CARBON DIOXIDE stays in the atmosphere for hundreds or thousands of years, simply stopping emissions is not enough. We need to draw carbon out of the atmosphere. Remember the overflowing bathtub? Once we stop adding water, we still need to remove some to reduce it to a safe level. With carbon dioxide, that safe level is below 350 ppm. To reduce 1 ppm of carbon dioxide in the atmosphere, we need to remove (draw down) 2.12 gigatons of carbon and store it somewhere. To reduce the 2021 predicted average atmospheric carbon dioxide concentration of 416 ppm to 350 ppm, we need to remove and store more than 140 gigatons of carbon. The longer we wait, the more carbon dioxide there will be, and the more work and money it will take to get it out.

There's lots of talk about geoengineering solutions to suck carbon dioxide out of the atmosphere, such as seeding the ocean with iron to stimulate photosynthesis by phytoplankton, or shielding the planet from incoming solar radiation by spraying chemicals in the atmosphere. Some forms of carbon capture and storage are already being used. So far none of these geoengineering schemes work on a large-enough scale to do the job fast enough, many are prohibitively expensive, some simply mask the problem, and there's always the potential for serious negative unintended consequences.

Nature has the answer. Drawing carbon dioxide out of the atmosphere is most efficiently done by photosynthesis—in other words, plant growth on land and in the ocean. Plants remove atmospheric carbon dioxide during photosynthesis to build their carbon-based structures, but they also transfer 40 percent of the carbon into soil, where it is stored for hundreds of years. Encouraging the growth of plants that are especially good at absorbing and storing carbon, such as forests, grasslands, seagrass ecosystems, kelp and mangrove forests, is a nature-based, or natural climate, solution. Nature-based solutions are among the fastest ways to solve the problem. They also have many co-benefits for biodiversity and human lives. Nature-based solutions remind us that humanity is a part of nature and intricately bound up with it.

Nature-based solutions to the climate crisis relate to changing the ways we use land and water and produce food. Human activities such as mining, forestry, industrial agriculture, urban and nearshore development and overfishing have destroyed or damaged half of the planet's mangrove swamps, about 70 percent of the wetlands, up to a third of the grasslands and half of the area of forest. These ecosystems are all natural carbon sinks, which means they absorb and store carbon. If damaged to a great-enough extent, they can become carbon sources. Ecosystem destruction may have as great an impact and contribute as much to global heating as burning fossil fuels. For example, deforestation leads to drought, wetland destruction reduces water availability, and removal of mangroves increases storm damage to coastal land.

The loss of ecosystems and their ability to sequester carbon is making the climate crisis worse. And the changing climate itself is causing more damage to these vital ecosystems through wildfires, megastorms, drought, sea level rise and ocean heating and acidification. We need to stop the damage and help ecosystems recover. We can do this by protecting and restoring nature, and by shifting to agricultural practices that regenerate rather than diminish soil health.

PROTECTION

NATURE CAN RECOVER IF given the chance. Protecting it from further damage is the first step.

It makes sense to stop logging, mining, drilling, building on and plowing up all primary (undamaged) forests, wetlands and nearshore ecosystems, and then protect them from any future activity of this kind. The International Union for Conservation of Nature (IUCN) defines a protected area as "a clearly defined geographical space, recognized, dedicated and managed, through legal or other effective means, to achieve the long-term conservation of nature with associated ecosystem services and cultural values." National parks, wilderness areas, community conserved areas and nature reserves are all examples of protected areas.

As of 2021, about 17 percent of the world's land and 8 percent of the ocean is protected through various programs, although not all protected areas are large enough or managed in such a way as to ensure adequate conservation of biodiversity. When it comes to protected areas, bigger is better! They need to be placed where they are most beneficial, and be interconnected and linked by habitat corridors to allow plants and animals to move as the climate changes. To be truly protected, they need to be off-limits to industrial activity, including oil and gas exploration and extraction, commercial fishing and seabed mining.

Ecologist and author E.O. Wilson started the Half-Earth Project to promote protecting half of the planet's land and ocean area. It's a bold plan but may be what's needed to solve the climate crisis. The current global network of protected areas stores at least 15 percent of terrestrial carbon. According to Project Drawdown, completely protecting Earth's remaining large primary ecosystems, such as the boreal forest in the north and the Amazon rainforest—both considered global treasures—along with most coastal and ocean ecosystems would draw down and store up to 10 gigatons of carbon by 2050. Another similar initiative, Nature Needs Half, is a coalition of conservationists and conservation organizations committed to "protecting 50 percent of Earth by 2030 for the benefit of all life."

ECOLOGIST E.O. WILSON IS A CLIMATE HERO!

He started the Half Earth Project to protect half of Earth's land and ocean area to ensure sufficient biodiversity to maintain the planet's health.

But half for nature will only work if people are part of the plan, especially the world's small-scale farmers and Indigenous Peoples, who live close to the land and who rely on nature most. Co-management of protected areas with local communities and Indigenous groups is becoming more common. Some protected areas, such as tribal parks, allow local Indigenous communities to hunt and gather traditional foods and practice cultural traditions. Carbon offset programs such as Carbon Landscapes pay communities to protect forests rather than cut them down for firewood or clear them to grow food, thereby protecting ecosystems while supporting the people who most depend on them. It's important to regulate and manage carbon offset programs carefully so they don't become an excuse to pollute. The forgiveness of debt owed to the World Bank by developing countries, in exchange for the protection of important ecosystems, has been suggested as a creative way to encourage conservation in jurisdictions often forced to liquidate nature to repay their debts.

RESTORATION

RELYING ON ECOSYSTEMS TO draw down carbon from the atmosphere will only work if they are healthy enough to function properly. The United Nations has declared 2021 to 2030 the Decade on Ecosystem Restoration. Restoration is the practice of returning an ecosystem to a state where natural processes can once again provide clean air and fresh water, quality wildlife habitat, carbon sequestration and other benefits for humans and wildlife alike.

Restoring carbon-rich ecosystems, on a large or small scale, in rural or urban settings, has the potential to remove large amounts of greenhouse gases from the atmosphere and store them for long periods. One recent study calculated that reforesting previously treed areas around the world (excluding cities and farms) could create about 1 billion additional hectares (2.5 billion acres) of forest with the potential to draw down and store one- to two-thirds of the extra carbon we've emitted since pre-industrial times. Healthy seagrass ecosystems can store more carbon dioxide per hectare than forests.

Large restoration projects, especially reforestation, are happening in many countries. In 2019 more than a million volunteers in India planted over 220 million trees in one day to tackle the climate crisis and improve the environment. Of course, it's important to plant the right trees in the right places to ensure success.

This reforestation project in Brazil, with vegetable beds planted between trees, Is a good example of regenerative agriculture.

REGENERATION

FEEDING ALL OF US globally accounts for a whopping quarter of anthropogenic greenhouse gas emissions. In addition, habitat loss and damage from land clearing and cultivation, and the use of chemical fertilizers and pesticides, have led to declining wildlife populations, polluted water sources and dead zones, decreased soil fertility and reduced soil carbon. Growing food in a regenerative way that works with nature to restore and enhance land, increase biodiversity and build soil health reduces emissions and increases carbon sequestration. Studies show that regenerative organic farming, also known as agroecology, can produce similar yields to conventional farming. Regenerative methods include, for example, no-till organic manure systems, permaculture, managed grazing to sequester carbon in grassland soils, and improved rice cultivation to prevent the production of methane.

To help make the needed transition, subsidies currently given to conventional farming could be redirected to help farmers transition to regenerative farming and help connect young farmers to the land. How about international *fair* trade rather than *free* trade treaties to protect local agricultural economies?

WHAT CAN YOU DO?

PROTECTING ECOSYSTEMS ON A large-enough scale to get us back to 350 ppm needs to be done by government and the big conservation organizations, but you can support their efforts through encouragement, volunteering and donations. At the local level, join your community conservation organization (or create one) to protect those carbon-rich ecosystems closest to home. My community raised over half a million dollars, mostly in small donations, to protect a 16-hectare (41-acre) forested nature reserve and the plants and animals that live there. You can even advance the protection of land by eating a plant-based diet. Growing plant crops uses less land than raising livestock, leaving more land to be returned to nature.

You can give nature a hand at recovery. Local restoration projects are always looking for volunteers. Check out Ecosystem Restoration Camps, a nonprofit organization in the Netherlands that organizes restoration camps around the world. I work for a small nonprofit organization that restores marine eelgrass ecosystems. We couldn't do the work without volunteers, and we have a lot of fun doing it too.

Ben Slattery from Australia and Rachel Dyer from the UK are learning how to grow food regeneratively on a small farm in Canada as WWOOFers with World Wide Opportunities on Organic Farms.

Support regenerative agriculture by choosing organic foods grown without pesticides and chemical fertilizers and in a way that enhances soil health. Educate yourself about regenerative methods and practice them by starting your own garden or participating in a local community garden. As an added benefit, buying locally grown food supports your local community.

Biophilia is the innate connection we humans have with other living organisms. Getting our hands dirty (and wet) by planting trees on previously deforested land, restoring nearshore ecosystems, *rewilding*, or

growing food using practices that restore soil health not only draws down carbon and supports biodiversity, but also helps us reconnect with each other and the natural world. Studies have shown that when we feel more connected to nature, we are more motivated to protect it.

TRANSITION TO CLEAN RENEWABLE ENERGY

Growing fruit and vegetables organically in your own garden or buying them from farms that practice regenerative agriculture is a form of climate action. Eat the food you enjoy, but do it mindfully. *How Bad Are Bananas? The Carbon Footprint of Everything* by Mike Berners-Lee is a great resource for educating yourself about food choices.

MAGINE HOW FAST the world could *decarbonize* from a fossil fuel economy to a clean-energy economy if all the money given every year to fossil fuel companies was directed toward renewable-energy projects, mass transit and energy refits for buildings. In 2009 Dr. Mark Jacobson of Stanford University wrote a paper that described how the world can supply all its energy needs by 2050 using a mix of wind, water and solar power, combined with energy efficiency. Then in 2011 he helped start The Solutions Project, which provides grants and support to grassroots climate changemakers and others to aid the global transition to 100 percent renewable energy. You can visit the "Our 100% Clean Energy Vision" page on the website and click on the interactive map to find out how the transition can happen in your city or country. You'll also see how your region can benefit in terms of healthcare and energy costs, land use and employment. For the entire world, the Solutions Project shows that the transition to 100 percent wind, water and solar energy, combined with improved energy efficiency, would create 55 million good long-term jobs, reduce energy demand by 57 percent, save $30 trillion in healthcare costs and require less than 1 percent of the planet's land area.

BedZed, completed in 2002, is the United Kingdom's first large-scale zero-carbon eco-village. It includes 100 homes, office space, a college and community facilities.

DO WE NEED NUCLEAR POWER?

THE WORD *NUCLEAR* makes a lot of baby boomers like me nervous. We grew up during the time of the Cold War and the Chernobyl nuclear disaster. We were as worried then about nuclear war and accidents as we are now about global heating.

Several people whose climate work I greatly admire argue that the world needs what are known as Generation IV nuclear reactors. Their reasoning is that fossil fuels, particularly coal, are damaging the planet so badly, and killing so many people every year (air pollution alone contributes to at least seven million deaths worldwide annually), we need to put aside our prejudices against nuclear power and embrace it as a bridge to a clean-energy future. It's true that nuclear power produces an enormous amount of zero-emission power. A lump of uranium the size of a golf ball can produce clean energy for an average person's lifetime. Advocates claim that the new generation of reactors no longer has the waste problem (they burn existing nuclear waste and can use stable fuel alternatives like thorium), the accident problem (they operate at low pressure) and the weapons problem (no or little weapons-grade plutonium is produced). Scalable and modular, they are compatible with decentralized local electricity grids.

Critics argue that the technology is too expensive, requires mining and fossil fuels to build, is not renewable, still produces radioactive waste, will distract us from the needed system change and could have unintended consequences. I still get a knot in my stomach when I think about nuclear energy, but I want to be open-minded. It may not matter what I think, though, because research and development of Generation IV reactors is well underway.

The transition is starting to happen. According to the International Renewable Energy Agency, two-thirds of power-production capacity added in 2018 was from renewables, mostly wind and solar. In 2019 Britain produced more electricity from renewable sources than from fossil fuels, and in 2020 Scotland produced 100 percent of its electricity with renewables, mostly wind power. In 2019 Costa Rica announced a plan to get to net-zero emissions by 2050.

One of the big advantages of generating electricity using renewable-energy sources like wind and solar is that such systems can easily be installed on a small scale in homes and communities. My friends Tom Mommsen and Risa Smith started the Salish Sea Renewable Energy Co-op (SSREC) to support the installation of low-carbon energy systems at homes, businesses and community facilities in their region. Within the first year and a half, SSREC had 165 members and had installed a total of 650 kilowatts of solar energy capacity in some 83 systems, resulting in total annual savings of about 420 metric tons of carbon dioxide. Small-scale systems like those created by SSREC help reduce the need for large power plants, and when such *distributed energy* is combined with local battery storage, they provide individuals and communities with local control over energy generation and some energy self-sufficiency in the case of a power-grid outage.

This is particularly advantageous for developing nations, where many people and communities have never had electricity and all the benefits that go along with it. These jurisdictions can leapfrog over large, expensive power plants and distribution networks and go directly to small-scale solar and wind installations, exemplified by the recent growth in largely off-grid mini- and micro-grids. Off-grid solar home systems consist of small photovoltaic arrays with limited battery storage to power small appliances. Tiny pico-solar systems,

Small solar installations allow people who have never had access to electricity, as in this informal settlement in South Africa, to power their homes for the first time.

where a low-power solar panel (in the 11-watt range) is coupled with a small battery, a light-emitting diode and a USB port, can light up homes and charge cell phones and laptops cheaply and efficiently. It makes sense for the countries that industrialized first and are most responsible for the climate crisis to help fund the adoption of renewable energy by developing countries. And since greenhouse gases know no boundaries, it benefits everyone.

Powering the electrical grid with renewables and electrifying transportation will go a long way toward cutting emissions. The cost of producing energy with renewables, especially solar, has dropped dramatically, to the point where it is cheaper than producing the equivalent energy using fossil fuels, hydro or nuclear power. As Tom and Risa say, "Fossil fuels are dead. Even without the climate crisis, renewable energy makes sense for lots of reasons." Other benefits of kicking our fossil fuel habit, besides lower costs, include clean air and water and reduced conflict over oil, gas and coal resources.

How are we going to pay for the transition? Diverting subsidies from fossil fuels is one way. Creating community and public banks is another way. Public banks can create money to be used for social good rather than for profit. The Sparkassen savings banks in Germany and the Infrastructure Development Company in Bangladesh are examples of public banks that provide low-interest or interest-free loans to finance the installation of clean energy for homes, businesses and communities. Pollution taxes, deposit-return systems for reusable and recyclable products, and tariffs on imported high-carbon goods could all be used to raise money for the transition. Imagine how much money could be freed up by demilitarizing society.

THE LOW-CARBON CITY

CITIES, BECAUSE THEY ARE where most of the planet's inhabitants live and work, have huge potential to advance the transition toward a low-carbon economy. More than any other level of government, cities are declaring climate emergencies, making climate pledges and taking real action. Getting people out of their cars and onto renewable-powered mass transit, into electric vehicles, onto bicycles and e-bikes, and walking is an important step (pun intended). City design and land-use planning can create opportunities for citizens to make low-carbon and ecologically sound choices. How about free bus passes for everyone under 25? (Did I hear a resounding cheer?) Concentrating the population in compact, walkable urban centers with a good public-transit system would mean that many residents don't need a vehicle.

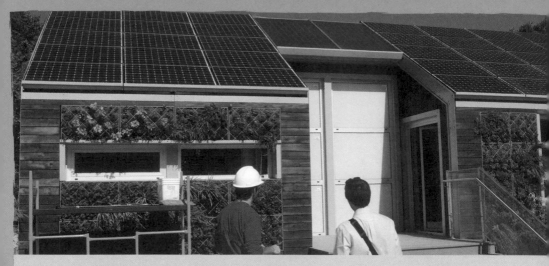

The plants on the walls of this passive house are fed with the waste (gray) water produced within the home, a brilliant natural waste-management solution.

Requiring new buildings to be energy efficient, even zero-emission, and providing subsidies or tax incentives to retrofit older buildings not only reduces reliance on energy but also reduces costs for the owner or tenant. *Passive homes* use 90 percent less energy than conventional homes, which can be retrofitted to the same standard. Brussels, Belgium, has required passive design standards for new homes and retrofits since 2015.

Many cities are relaxing or changing regulations in order to encourage urban gardening and farming, promote the installation of renewable-energy systems at homes and businesses, and allow nonconventional businesses such as ride- and accommodation-sharing to operate. Governments can help by bringing in policies to make it easier for their citizens to make zero- or low-emission choices, such as rebates for installing solar panels or loans to support community food-security programs.

The co-benefits are enormous. Zero-emission cities and towns have clean air and water, a more active population and better social cohesion through community participation.

- CAR-FREE CITY -

DURING THE COVID-19 PANDEMIC we got a taste of cities without cars. Many people commented how quiet and less polluted their urban neighborhoods became. Now stretch your imagination further. The roads in a city car-free by design are narrower or have been replaced with food and pollinator gardens, pedestrian walkways, bicycle paths and public squares and markets. Everyone is walking or cycling, so there's more opportunity to socialize with your neighbors. You get more exercise. The hassle of finding and paying for parking is gone. There's lots more room to plant trees, which absorb carbon dioxide, release oxygen and provide shade protection from summer sun. Electric buses, trains, taxis or car-shares travel in dedicated transportation corridors to take you where you need to go.

WHAT CAN YOU DO?

THERE ARE LOTS OF things you can do at the municipal level to encourage and support your community's efforts to transition to a low-carbon economy. After all, it's where you live. In fact, the community level is where citizens have the most influence. Encourage your municipal leaders to make the transition. Talk to them directly. Participate in community planning initiatives by attending community meetings, speaking up or filling out questionnaires to let your representatives know what you want them to do. Many municipalities have youth advisory forums that invite youth to participate directly in planning activities. I spoke with high school student Daylen Sawchuk, whose school Green Team is helping plan a large low-carbon development in his city. Get involved in community groups that advocate for local change. Use your community's public transportation network. Join a community garden or help set one up. The possibilities are as numerous as the people in your community. But using less energy is one of the main keys to making the transition to clean energy work.

Schools and community centers are ideal places for small distributed-energy systems. How about raising money to put solar panels on your school's roof? Once your family learns that renewable energy can save them money and create a healthier environment, maybe they'll consider installing a solar, wind or geothermal system to heat and power your home. A few years ago my husband and I installed solar panels on the roof of our house. They produce most of our spring-to-fall household electricity needs and charge our electric car. The cost of the system will be paid back to us in energy savings in a relatively short time. In some areas it's possible to rent a solar home system to reduce your electrical bill. Government rent-a-roof programs, where utility companies rent roof space on private homes and businesses to install solar panels and then sell the power back to them, offer an innovative way to promote the transition to renewable energy.

Repair cafés, like this one in Belfast, Ireland, are community meeting places equipped with tools, materials and expert help where you can repair your broken items together. There are 1,500 official repair cafés worldwide. How about a repair café for the planet?

CONSUME LESS

AS YOU READ in chapter 3, one of the main underlying causes of the climate crisis is our cultural addiction to perpetual growth. Degrowth is a critique of growth. It emphasizes using fewer natural resources and nurturing societies organized around sharing, simplicity, cooperation and caring for other people and the natural world. A degrowth world is well suited to a renewable-energy economy, which is by necessity a lower-energy economy than a fossil fuel one and therefore will be a smaller economy.

What does a degrowth world look like? It isn't about hardship and sacrifice. It's about living more simply and making quality of life the priority rather than quantity of stuff. It can even be fun. It's about increasing our "caring capacity." Canadian environmentalist Guy Dauncey calls this type of system the "economy of kindness." Think community gardens, vacant-lot gardening, work sharing, working less, reduced income but more freedom, community bike shops, repair cafés, energy cooperatives, volunteer work, local currencies, local exchange trading systems, local lending, guaranteed minimum income and citizens' assemblies. Seems to me that most, if not all, of these are already emerging as individuals and communities take up the slack left by governments to create the world they want to see.

Degrowth philosophy says the transition to a *steady-state economy* (one that operates within natural limits) needs to be driven from the bottom up rather than imposed from the top down. Buen vivir in Latin America, sumac kaway in Ecuador, economy of permanence in India and ubuntu in South Africa are all examples of philosophies that promote degrowth principles to enhance the lives of the citizens.

WHAT CAN YOU DO?

YOU MIGHT HAVE HEARD the sentiment that individual lifestyle choices won't make any difference to greenhouse gas emissions because the majority of emissions are produced by 100 corporations. Remember the bathtub analogy? Even one drop at a time will eventually fill that tub to overflowing. Personal emissions not only move the planet in the direction of more dangerous warming, but they also contribute to the bottom-line profits of those 100 corporations. And corporations are made up of individual people who value the well-being of their loved ones. You do have the power to influence what happens at corporate and government levels. Even if you are too young to vote and have limited funds, you can still vote with your actions and your wallet in some areas of your life, such as how you travel and how much, what you eat, and what and how many consumer goods you buy. And don't forget those co-benefits. Clean, green choices are good for your mental and physical health.

While you, as a young person, may not have directly caused the climate crisis, you are still entangled in the global fossil fuel–driven system along with everyone else on the planet. All of us are connected to it to different degrees. The key is to figure out how, and by how much, you can disentangle yourself from it.

US, Canadian and Australian per capita carbon dioxide emissions (from the burning of fossil fuels for energy and cement production) were about 16 tonnes (17.6 tons) in 2019—more than three times the global average. The average American emits as much carbon dioxide in seven days as the average Kenyan emits in one year. Who needs to reduce their emissions more? The recommended goal is personal carbon emissions of no more than 2 metric tons per year. There are several online carbon calculators you can use to find out what your carbon footprint is and where you can make the most effective cuts.

> The key is to figure out how, and by how much, you can disentangle.

In the same way a municipality might create a carbon-reduction plan, individuals are creating personal or group climate action plans. Jonathan Safran Foer, author of *We Are the Weather: Saving the Planet Begins at Breakfast*, carries his, on a piece of paper tucked into his pocket, everywhere he goes. Mine is in my head but includes things like fly no more than once a year to visit my mother, eat more vegetarian meals (less meat), grow more food and write this book. Your personal climate action plan might start with something simple like walking to school instead of driving, turning down the heat in the house, eating a vegetarian meal twice a week or keeping your cell phone until it dies (and then recycling it). You may not always stick to your plan. That's okay. It's not a contest. Every little bit counts. But an articulated action plan will help guide your daily choices.

Less is the key. Flying less, driving less, buying less, eating less meat and deciding to have fewer children are important personal choices that will make a big difference to greenhouse gas emissions if enough of us take the initiative. Earth Guardians' EarthTracks app lets you join the global community to support one another in making meaningful changes.

UNITE WITH AND LEARN FROM INDIGENOUS PEOPLES

THE WORLD HAS much to learn from Indigenous Peoples, who have lived on the land for thousands of years. They have learned to live in harmony with nature. Many Indigenous philosophies see humans as part of the interconnected whole of nature and believe humans are obligated to take care of it—a philosophy I share. Indigenous Peoples have learned to recover from past disruptions, whether caused by natural disasters or colonization and racist government policies and actions. Those who still live close to nature and rely on it for their daily well-being have been the first to notice the impact of changes in the climate, such as the loss of sea ice or the appearance of unusual plants or animals. They've been warning the world about changes in the climate for a long time.

TSLEIL-WAUTUTH NATION IS A CHANGEMAKER!

Their Administration and Health Centre solar panel array consists of approximately 350 solar photovoltaic panels capable of producing an estimated 150,000 kWh of electricity annually that will help offset energy use from this building. The project was partially funded by the BC Indigenous Clean Energy Initiative.

Modern civilization was built on the backs of Indigenous Peoples. It's still happening. Indigenous communities are often among those most affected by fossil fuel extraction and production in their traditional territories and are among the first to suffer from changes in climate, even though they have contributed little to cause it. Indigenous Peoples, communities and organizations around the world have been leading the fight against fossil fuel corporations and the politicians who enable them. Some have died for their efforts. In her book *On Fire: The (Burning) Case for a Green New Deal*, Naomi Klein argues that Indigenous communities on the front lines of the movement opposed to polluting, destructive industries should be the first to receive public support for clean-energy projects, many of which are already Indigenous-led.

Article 8(j) of the United Nations Convention on Biological Diversity encourages governments to "respect, preserve and maintain the knowledge, innovations and practices of Indigenous peoples and local communities relevant for the conservation and sustainable use of biological diversity." Indigenous Traditional Knowledge (ITK) is increasingly recognized to be complementary, sometimes superior, to Western science, offering another way of being and seeing the world. ITK—for example, Elders' stories and Oral Traditions—is now being incorporated into, or used instead of, Western methodologies of study, and collaborations with Indigenous people and communities as partners in scientific and monitoring programs are becoming common.

The adoption of the United Nations Declaration on the Rights of Indigenous Peoples in 2007 is an exciting step toward reconciling past harms and supporting Indigenous Peoples worldwide in their struggles for equality, although many jurisdictions have not signed it, and injustices continue. Sharing governance with Indigenous Peoples, at all levels and in all facets of life, is the right thing to do. It's also necessary. Indigenous Peoples make up less than 5 percent of the world's population, but their traditional territories support 80 percent of the world's biodiversity and store close to a quarter of the carbon stores in the world's tropical forests. Successful initiatives to address the climate crisis will need meaningful and respectful partnerships with Indigenous Peoples.

WHAT CAN YOU DO?

A GOOD PLACE TO start is to read the United Nations Declaration on the Rights of Indigenous Peoples. If you aren't Indigenous, find out about Indigenous communities near you. Know the history of the country you live in and understand the injustices that Indigenous Peoples there have experienced and continue to experience at the hands of the colonial governments still in charge. Look for opportunities to learn from Indigenous knowledge holders. Get to know your Indigenous neighbors. Support Indigenous communities in their struggles against the fossil fuel industry, and attend Indigenous-led climate actions.

DO NO HARM (OR AS LITTLE AS POSSIBLE)

ANY SOLUTION TO the climate crisis must be ecologically sound and equitable. Let's call equity and ecology our two solution lenses. If a solution ends up destroying more land or polluting water or displacing a community, it's not a real solution. Because everything is connected to everything else, actions that meet the two criteria will naturally lead to a reduction in greenhouse gas pollution and an increase in healthier ecosystems.

Take transportation, for example. Electrifying transportation and powering it with renewable energy will clean up air pollution and reduce greenhouse gases significantly, but the components, particularly storage batteries, require minerals such as cobalt, nickel, graphite, lithium, rare earths and aluminum. The need for these "green"-economy minerals is fueling a new resources rush that all too often tramples ecosystems and human rights. Many green-economy minerals are found in countries with fragile governments more prone to corruption, conflict and human-rights abuses.

It doesn't have to be that way. Demanding transparency (publishing where and how source materials are obtained); creating responsible international mining standards, regulations and oversight; and implementing better recycling and reuse requirements are all ways to clean up the supply chains. Some companies are taking on the challenge. Will we see ethically sourced certification labels on electric cars, solar panels and cell phones soon?

Programs to protect and restore nature can be problematic too. In 2008 the United Nations launched a program known as REDD,

THE CLIMATE JUSTICE ALLIANCE IS A CHANGEMAKER!

The coalition of rural and urban frontline communities, organizations and supporting networks works to build a just transition to a resilient, regenerative and equitable world.

which stands for "reducing emissions from deforestation and forest degradation." The program aims to reduce carbon emissions by encouraging developing countries to protect and sustainably manage their forests (soils and agriculture were added later) through carbon trading or payments for forest management. Sounds like a good nature-based solution, right? It can be, and many successful projects are listed on the UN-REDD website. But the Indigenous Environmental Network (IEN) argues that REDD is a new form of colonialism, referring to it as "reaping profits from evictions, land grabs, deforestation and destruction of biodiversity." The IEN project Global Alliance Against REDD cites examples of evictions, servitude, slavery, persecutions, killings, imprisonment and other abuses resulting from REDD and other carbon-forest projects. More and better regulations and oversight are necessary. Local and Indigenous communities need to be involved in planning, implementing and managing projects from the very start for those projects to be truly beneficial and fair.

A just transition to a clean economy will also require moral and financial support to retrain fossil fuel, forestry and agricultural workers whose jobs will disappear as we switch to renewable energy and regenerative agriculture.

WHAT CAN YOU DO?

EVERYTHING YOU DO HAS a consequence. Even reducing your consumption affects the livelihood of someone somewhere. To guide your personal choices, use the ecology and equity lenses. Is the laptop you need for school made with *conflict minerals*? Is that pair of jeans you want to buy made in a sweatshop halfway around the world? If the information that would help you make such decisions isn't available, demand transparency from government, manufacturers and sellers. Support and participate in the circular economy, which promotes consumer goods that are produced to last a long time and can be repaired, repurposed or recycled easily.

Considering ecology and equity when making purchases will ensure you aren't supporting unjust or environmentally harmful industries such as this shoe sweatshop in Thailand.

- MORE THAN GOLD -

Long ago in times of old
There lay a land now long untold;
A place that does within us hide,
A world worth far much more than gold.

The trees they blossomed in the spring,
The birds they flew on wind and wing,
And all about you felt a stir
As if the very earth could sing.

Yet in this peace a greed we knew,
We let it take us and it grew.
We turned away from change and truth
And named the fools the wise ones too.

Our homes were shattered into dust,
Our faces stained with tears and rust.
The closing time for change we missed
And lost our children's dreams and trust.

Long ago in times of old
There lay a land now long untold;
A place that does within us hide,
A world worth far much more than gold.

—Faith Kingsley

Faith Kingsley, *19, from Pennsylvania, hopes the climate emergency will be stopped as soon as possible so she can spend more time creating art, writing, making music, connecting with friends and nature, and daydreaming. In the meantime, she is trying her best to incorporate her hobbies into various forms of climate action.*

— 6 —

WHAT IF...
JUST IN CASE

How to Live in a Changing and Uncertain World

"We are not here to save the world,
only belong to it more fully."

—AUTHOR UNKNOWN

———

"Prepare to live in an age of uncertainty,
remind yourself our ancestors did just that,
and find a new, deeper meaning to life."

—DR. WOLFGANG KNORR,
CLIMATE SCIENTIST AND AUTHOR

SO HOW ARE we doing? First the good news. As you've learned, lots of people are making huge efforts to counter the climate crisis. Whole countries are declaring climate emergencies, setting dramatic goals to decarbonize and switch to renewables. Some corporations are stepping up and making changes to the carbon-intensive way they do business. Divestment from the fossil fuel industry by banks, universities and even whole countries has increased. Renewables are getting cheaper and more efficient. Cities and towns are increasing mass transit, putting electric buses on the road, building cycling lanes and refitting buildings to be more energy efficient. Individuals, families and communities are making daily low-carbon choices in the way they eat, make purchases and move around. Trees are being planted, and ecosystems are being restored. Millions are out in the streets, calling on leaders to take meaningful action.

But is it working fast enough to prevent the worst consequences of the changing climate? To be on track, we needed to start seeing a reduction in global greenhouse gas emissions by 2020. Are global greenhouse gas emissions dropping? Is the Keeling Curve starting to bend down toward zero? While global emissions did drop in 2020, the reason wasn't our collective climate actions but a decrease in travel and economic activity resulting from the COVID-19 pandemic. As pandemic restrictions eased, emissions rebounded. The bottom line: the global average temperature continues to rise. We have not yet been able to bend the atmospheric carbon curve enough to cool the planet. We also know that because of lags in the climate system, the climate will continue to change for a long time even after emissions are reduced. This means we will face increasingly challenging climatic disruptions in the future.

The volunteer fire department in my rural community is always urging us to be prepared for emergencies. "Get your grab-and-go bag

GRANDMA SURVIVED THE GREAT DEPRESSION

BECAUSE HER SUPPLY CHAIN WAS LOCAL

AND SHE KNEW HOW TO DO STUFF

ready, with copies of all your important papers, medications, phone numbers, clothes, a flashlight and enough food and water to last you for a few days." People who are prepared are better able to take care of themselves and their loved ones. Preparing for an emergency does not necessarily mean one is inevitable, but it can be reassuring to know you are ready if disaster occurs.

But how do we prepare for an emergency as huge as the climate crisis, which will affect so many people in so many ways, on both emotional and physical levels? The global COVID-19 pandemic may have given you some practice in thinking about some of these questions: What do you need to do to prepare for what's coming? What is your role in the world? Which of your skills and gifts are needed right now? What skills might you need to develop? How will you look after yourself emotionally in the face of difficult times? Will you choose to live in fear or in joy?

In this chapter, you'll hear how the scientists, environmentalists, artists, writers, Indigenous people, youth and many others I encountered in the course of my research answered these questions in relation to the climate crisis. Maybe you'll find something in their stories that will help you "weather the storm," help those around you and find pleasure in your daily life in spite of future predictions. The Resources section in this book also lists books and websites full of information that will help you prepare.

LEARN TO DO STUFF

WHAT WILL YOU need to know if the outside sources of food, medicine and other consumer goods are no longer available? If the electricity goes out? If a climate migrant comes knocking on your door? I asked everyone I interviewed to suggest practical skills to learn for staying healthy and safe in turbulent times. Here's what they suggested.

To keep fed and physically healthy, learn how to:

- Grow food sustainably wherever you live
- Cook, prepare and preserve food
- Milk a cow or goat
- Cook on a fire (and start one!)
- Collect and purify water
- Forage for wild food
- Grow, prepare and eat insects

To keep things working, learn how to:

- Respect and use tools
- Plumb and install electrical wiring
- Work with wood
- Sew, knit, crochet and quilt
- Make shoes
- Cooper (barrel making)
- Make candles
- Build and fire pottery
- Live without electricity
- Live cell phone–free

To stay safe, learn:

- First aid
- Preventative medicine
- To care for a sick person
- To recognize medicinal plants and make herbal remedies
- Firefighting
- Survival skills such as shelter building and navigation
- Self-defense

To stay connected to others, learn:

- Nonviolent communication and how to get along with others, including strangers

- Indigenous wisdom about living in harmony with nature

- Community organizing

- Community building

This might seem like a long, if incomplete, list. Start with one skill and see where it takes you. Community centers often have skills-based courses. Or seek out mentors among your friends and family. Asking them to share their knowledge might just improve their mental health too. People like to know they are needed. Maybe you'll be asked to mentor someone else. And if the world manages to avert disaster, well, you'll know how to do a lot of valuable things.

CONNECT WITH NATURE

WHEN I ASKED people how they look after themselves when the news about the climate crisis seems overwhelming, or they are feeling exhausted from working hard to change the situation, most of them put spending time in nature at or near the top of their list. Sam leaves his cell phone at home and goes to a special bench in the forest when he feels overwhelmed. Tessa helps her grandmother work in her organic garden. She loves the feel of the soil in her hands. Sandy goes swimming in the ocean. Charlotte spends time with her animals. Grace walks in the forest or on the beach. I paddle my kayak on the ocean.

Not everyone lives where nature is easily accessible, but even watching urban birds or growing a plant in your house connects you with other species we share the planet with. Look for opportunities to learn about the plants, animals and ecosystems around you.

Taking a breath of air or a drink of water with awareness connects you to nature in the simplest, most basic of ways, reminding you that you are a part of nature and rely on it for your very existence.

MAKE ROOM FOR SILENCE

MANY OF US live busy lives, studying, working, socializing, volunteering, saving the world. Making space in the day for silence is a way many people turn off the outside world and cultivate a sense of calm. Several of the young people I interviewed told me how much their cell phones and social media have taken over their lives and that they consciously turn them off now and then to give themselves a break. Many people told me they spend time sitting silently in nature to ground themselves.

Silence can also help you develop the ability to "be in the moment." When you are using your senses to see, hear, smell and feel your surroundings, it's less likely you'll be worrying about what might happen tomorrow or in 10 years or a hundred.

SELF-CARE: DO WHAT YOU LOVE

SPENDING TIME IN nature and making room for silence are ways to nurture yourself. Earth Guardian Sierra Robinson, who was finishing high school at the time I talked with her, organizes climate marches, teaches permaculture and is a plaintiff in a children's lawsuit against the Canadian government for climate inaction. She finds it easy to become exhausted and depressed. She said, "I can't give to my community if I don't look after myself." Her self-care practices to "lift the weight off my shoulders" are to spend time in nature, hang out with friends, write poetry, keep a journal and enjoy art and music.

Don't let your whole life be taken over by the climate crisis. Spend time doing what you love. People told me they ward off anxiety by writing stories and poems, meditating, journaling, dancing, practicing yoga, making art, doing crafts and going to museums, galleries, concerts and the theater. Maybe you love sports, reading or knitting. Spend time doing it every day. Or simply take a day or two off to kick back. The message is to maintain those activities in your life that give you meaning and fulfillment. And don't forget, eating a healthy diet and getting daily exercise and ample sleep are excellent ways to boost your mental health.

BURNING QUESTION

SHOULD I GET RID OF MY CELL PHONE?

MATERIAL OBJECTS ARE not inherently bad. It depends on how they are used, produced and disposed of. Cell phones are criticized for using energy, for being made from environmentally and socially destructive conflict minerals and oil products, for taking over people's lives and for filling up landfills when the next new model comes along. On the positive side, cell phones have improved the lives of many people in developing countries, who don't have access to telephones and electricity. They are useful in an emergency and effective in rallying support for climate strikes through social media. Cell phones are easily recharged using a portable solar charger. The more uses a cell phone has, the greener it is. For example, a cell phone can replace the carbon footprint of a flashlight, a clock, a computer, a calculator, a book and even a car if you use it to order online, watch a movie or read a book.

How can you be a "smart" phone owner? Purchase a used phone or one that's made in an environmentally sustainable and socially equitable manner. Keep your phone a long time and recycle it when its life is over. Use it to change the world, then turn it off and spend your time in nature or with your friends and family.

FEEL YOUR EMOTIONS

MY **FRIEND JANE** beats on a block of wood in her basement to let out her rage at the failure of the fossil fuel corporations and world leaders to act on the climate crisis. I laughed when she told me, but it's healthy for her to acknowledge her anger (she's also an awesome community organizer and supporter of youth activists). Youth have a lot to be angry about, especially their being left to deal with the environmental mess created by previous generations. It's okay to feel anger, grief, sadness, despair and helplessness. Feeling your emotions is good for your mental and physical health. Pushing them away or keeping them inside is usually not. Film creator Josh Fox, in his film *How to Let Go of the World and Love All the Things Climate Can't Change*, said he "had to make a place in my heart for despair. In turbulent times it becomes an anchor."

I already mentioned eco-anxiety, something many of us struggle with. Don't be alone with your emotions if they get overwhelming. Share them with trusted friends and family members, visit a counselor, or join a climate-anxiety support group in your community (or start one!).

It's healthy to acknowledge and express your emotions, and it's also healthy to nurture a positive outlook. After all, no one can predict the climate future, so why not choose the positive over the negative? Grace Nosek and her colleagues at the UBC Climate Hub actively nurture joy and agency in the young people they work with in their Youth Climate Ambassador program. They do this by storytelling, showing how other young folks are taking the lead on climate justice and taking action as a collective. And while it's good to keep informed, don't hesitate to step away from the television, the computer, the newspapers—and your phone—when the bad news becomes overwhelming. Kiersten Brookes, who teaches at a nature-based elementary school, follows the Good News Network on the internet and looks for examples of positive actions by others to help keep her spirits up. She and her young students channel their emotions into positive actions every day. In 2019 they created an environmental award for companies doing a good job of reducing their carbon emissions. Many recipients attended the ceremony to receive the award from the youth.

Calming activities like meditation or yoga are helpful forms of self-care.

NEED HELP WITH CLIMATE ANXIETY?

EXPERIENCING CLIMATE ANXIETY? Don't know where to turn? The Good Grief Network is ready to help. Its 10-step program aims "to help build personal resilience and empowerment while strengthening community ties to combat despair, inaction and eco-anxiety on the collective level." Groups meet online or in person in various locations in the United Kingdom, United States, Canada and Australia. If there's no meeting in your community, the network will help you start one.

Eco-Anxious Stories is another online community where you can share your experiences with others and support one another.

- GREEN REVOLUTION -

OUR FAMILY HAD always been relatively green: we were nature lovers, vegetarians, and tried to buy all-natural foods. We were that stereotypical green family, but in reality we were far from sustainable. We hadn't realized there was more to being green than recycling.

Our first eye-opener happened when my sister was 10. Her group of friends decided to sign up for the school's Green Team. So she did too. She learned about waste, emissions and the urgency of the climate crisis. She brought all of this home and got passionate to the point that she was mad if we didn't put our waste in the right bin.

She joined to have fun and came out as a climate activist.

At first I thought she was getting a little too crazy over this, but when it was my turn to join the Green Team, I caught the activism bug big-time. I suddenly understood the reality I was born into, and I was compelled to do something.

My family experienced a green transformation. We changed our lifestyle completely over the course of two years and even convinced our parents to buy an electric car! We are now nearly zero-waste, we have reduced our flying, almost all of us are vegan, we participate in local climate strikes and more. My sister and I now lead the Green Team with a few other involved students, as well as helping organize climate action events that the school runs.

In order to overcome the climate crisis, we need everyone on board. So join the revolution and make a change—no one is too small to make a difference!

—Gal Barnea

Gal Barnea, *13, organizes the annual Earth Day at her school in Montreal and runs the Green Team with some other students. She wants to become a climate scientist or activist (I think she already is one).*

Transition Network is a movement of thousands of groups in towns, cities, universities and schools in over 50 countries which are "reimaging and rebuilding (the) world." Greyton, the first Transition Town in Africa, has used profits from its Ecolodge and a vegetarian/vegan restaurant to turn a municipal dump into a green park, plant a 500-tree fruit forest, build an outdoor classroom with nonrecyclable plastic waste, and create organic permaculture food gardens at six schools.

JOIN A CLIMATE ACTION GROUP

EVERYONE I INTERVIEWED told me they felt more positive about the future when they were working with others to make a difference. There's no Superman or Superwoman out there, swooping in to rescue us from the bad guys—just a lot of people pooling their energy and talents. Even high-profile super-youth like Greta Thunberg, Jamie Margolin and Autumn Peltier have a lot of people in the background helping them. Gabe, a retired teacher who helped start a climate action group in his neighborhood, told me that the courage needed to confront the tough times ahead comes from working with others and discovering that the world needs your abilities.

Environmentalist Guy Dauncey says that he too wards off despair at the state of the world by taking action with others. "Action nurtures a sense of inner calm in the face of the crisis," he told me. He recommends finding or creating a group of at least five people who not only act together but also study the science and climate issues together. The knowledge you gain will give you more confidence to discuss the climate crisis with those people who don't agree with or understand the science. Guy also says, "If it's not fun, it's not sustainable."

BE IN CONTROL OF YOUR CHOICES

EVEN THOUGH INDIVIDUAL lifestyle choices to reduce carbon emissions can seem minuscule and inconsequential compared to the carbon footprints of huge fossil fuel corporations, being mindful of your own behavior and adjusting it, even in small increments, can help you feel more in control. Making the climate crisis a factor in your decisions about what to eat, how you get places, what you wear, what you buy and how you buy it can help relieve climate anxiety. After all, who else has the authority to make your choices but you? Don't beat yourself up if you fail to live up to your commitments. We're all doing our best. The important part is to have a sense of agency in your life.

DISABILITIES AND DISASTER PLANNING

PEOPLE WITH DISABILITIES are often at great disadvantage during a disaster. How do you escape a flood if you are in a wheelchair? Or avoid falling trees in a hurricane if you are blind? Rebuild your life after a disaster when your disability pension is barely enough to survive on in good times? The United Nations has directed governments to consider disabled people in planning for the climate crisis. Organizations such as Ready (ready.gov) provide planning guidance.

SEEK OUT A MENTOR

O **NE THING I** heard from adults during my research was that young people don't want help from them because the older generation is responsible for the climate crisis in the first place. It's an understandable sentiment, but the young activists I talked with said they were grateful for the help of the adults in their lives.

Many adults have been working for a long time on scores of the world's problems and have valuable skills and knowledge to share. Adult mentors Sandy, Susan and Jane sit quietly at the back of the

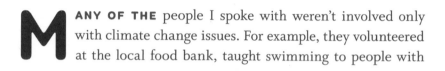

room during the local youth-led Earth Guardians meetings. The young people run the meetings and make the decisions. The adults are there to help when they are needed. Greta Thunberg asks climate scientists to review her speeches to make sure the science is correct, and she looks to adults to provide her with zero-emission transportation to get her to climate marches and global summits. Adults act as safety monitors during climate strikes, and bake cookies to help raise funds.

Who loves you the most? It's usually your parents/guardians and grandparents, isn't it? They've worked hard to keep you housed, fed and safe. A group of parents and grandparents in Canada started For Our Kids to take action to make sure their children and grandchildren have a livable future.

Intergenerational connections are often missing in our busy modern lives. Don't feel shy about seeking out supportive wise men and women. They just might be able to teach you some of the skills suggested. And they will certainly learn things from you. I sure learned a lot from the young people I interviewed.

GIVE BACK

MANY OF THE people I spoke with weren't involved only with climate change issues. For example, they volunteered at the local food bank, taught swimming to people with disabilities, read to schoolchildren or did crafts with seniors. Each of them said volunteering not only helped others, but also gave them a sense of purpose and belonging, which ultimately improved their outlook on the state of the world. Volunteering also better connected them with their neighbors, communities and the natural world.

Like these young dancers in St. Petersburg, Russia, supporting others to do what you all love will lift your spirits and expand your friendships.

PRACTICE GRATITUDE

GIVING BACK IS about stepping outside your normal sphere of activity, focusing less on yourself and more on others. Practicing gratitude is similar. Gratitude—feeling appreciation for things you have received from others—helps you recognize that you are part of an interconnected network that supports and nurtures you. Appreciating nature for providing you with healthy food, clean water and air, beauty, birds, butterflies and all the other ecosystem benefits is an important step toward developing the desire to take care of it. Author Dahr Jamail recommends that each of us find one place we love and look after it. Imagine what would happen if everyone took his advice.

- TREE HUGGER -

when i was two,
i would hug every tree
that i saw.

they say
that walking 5 blocks
took an hour, at least.

i hope that those
hundreds of squeezes
when i was a kid
make up, at least a bit,
for those 5,000-ish days
i forgot to say thanks.

—Gwynneth Tansey

Canadian poet **Gwynneth Tansey,** *18, has loved being in nature since she was little. Now she also likes finding ways to help people incorporate climate action into their everyday lives. No matter what she's doing, she's always thinking of ways to make it as sustainable as possible.*

A FINAL WORD

IN AUGUST 2021, as *Urgent Message* was about to go to press, the first of three new reports from the IPCC, *Climate Change 2021: The Physical Science Basis*, was released. While I didn't have time to incorporate all the new information, the message remains the same and is even more urgent. The climate crisis is getting worse, the planet's temperature increasing with every ton of greenhouse gas emitted to the atmosphere and with every bit of damage done to nature. We're pretty much guaranteed to exceed 1.5 °C of warming by 2040 or sooner. But we can still reduce the level of harm if we act quickly and coopera- tively to cut emissions and restore natural land and ocean carbon sinks. The report suggests that stopping emissions of short-lived, powerful greenhouse gases other than carbon dioxide, such as methane and nitrous oxide, might achieve significant results quickly. Are you ready to demand meaningful action? My protest signs are ready.

Researching and writing *Urgent Message* was not easy with all the difficult news and uncertainty. What kept me going was a word that I heard over and over as I talked with people about the climate crisis. That word was *gratitude*. I'm grateful I had the opportunity to contrib- ute to the conversation about the climate crisis by writing this book. I'm grateful for nature, which kept me going. I'm grateful to all the people I talked to and to those who wrote the books and articles I read during my research. I'm grateful to the youth who submitted stories, poems and visual art. I'm grateful to you for reading my book. Thank you!

Most of all, I'm grateful for the collective action that is welling up all over the world. Now is the time to act. Waiting will only make things worse. In the words of climate scientist Katharine Hayhoe, "The more we do, the better off we'll be."

ACKNOWLEDGMENTS

I **ACKNOWLEDGE WITH GRATITUDE** that I live, work and play on the traditional unceded territory of the Hul'qumi'num-speaking Coast Salish Indigenous Peoples.

Transforming the world will require everyone to work together. Creating a book often feels like it relies on almost as many people! Thank you to the dozens of people I interviewed—for your time, your knowledge and your valuable work to create a better planet. Your input and stories made the manuscript more compelling and complete. To the youth who submitted their stories, poems, artworks and photographs, you and your creative climate work are awesome! I am enormously grateful to expert reviewers Elizabeth Bagley from Project Drawdown, Ed Wiebe from the Faculty of Earth and Ocean Sciences at the University of Victoria, and Navin Ramankutty from the Institute of Resources, Environment and Sustainability at the University of British Columbia. Any errors are my own.

And what would I do without my thoughtful readers and their feedback on all or parts of the manuscript? Thank you Tory Stevens, Gary Geddes, Charlotte Fesnoux, Rina Nichols, Glen Woolaver, Lorne Underwood, Ed Wiebe, Tom Mommsen and Risa Smith. It's always a pleasure to work with my fabulous editor, Sarah Harvey. Thank you to Ruth Linka and Andrew Wooldridge at Orca Book Publishers for your support for my ideas and for making this book possible. My appreciation to the creative crew at Orca, who always produce books of the highest quality and make sure they get out into the world. To my literary agent, John Pearce: I value your friendship along with your efforts to find homes for my writing. To my family: your love and encouragement keep me going.

GLOSSARY

adaptation—the process of adjusting to changes in the environment

agroecology—a form of sustainable farming that uses ecological concepts in food production in order to minimize damage to ecosystems, biodiversity and human communities

albedo—the reflective power of a surface—a light surface has a higher albedo than a dark surface

amplifying feedback—a response to a small change in a system that increases (positive feedback) or decreases (negative feedback) the magnitude of the change

anthropogenic—caused by humans

biodiversity—the variety of life found in a particular ecosystem

biophilia—the innate urge in humans to engage with other forms of life

cap and trade—a system of carbon pricing that puts an upper limit on (caps) the amount of carbon a company can emit, but allows it to exceed that quota by buying emission rights from a company that hasn't used up its own quota

capitalism—an economic system in which the means of producing material goods and services are owned by private individuals or corporations, for the prime purpose of earning profit

carbon budget—the amount of carbon dioxide that can be emitted into Earth's atmosphere before reaching a certain threshold

carbon footprint—a measure of the greenhouse gas emissions caused by a person, group or product; see also *ecological footprint*

carbon sinks—things that absorb more carbon dioxide from Earth's atmosphere than they release—for example, soil, the ocean and plants

carbon sources—things that release carbon dioxide into Earth's atmosphere, such as wild-fires and cities

carbon tax (carbon fee)—a tax on energy sources that emit carbon dioxide, calculated on the carbon content of fuels (coal, oil, natural gas) and imposed to reduce carbon emissions

carrying capacity—the maximum population of a species that an ecosystem can support indefinitely

circular economy—an economic system designed to reduce waste and pollution and minimize the production of goods by reducing, reusing, refurbishing, repurposing and recycling products and materials

climate—the long-term average weather over a period of time, typically 30 years

climate anxiety—a feeling of worry and dread about the climate and ecological crisis

colonialism—the oppressive control and exploitation of one group of people by another

conflict minerals—minerals that are mined from areas of armed conflict, the profit from which is used to fund armed groups, and which are linked to human-rights abuses and environmental damage

deadly threshold—the point at which the combination of high temperature and humidity becomes lethal to humans

decarbonize—to remove carbon from a product, a process or an economy

desertification—the process of land becoming a desert as the result of human activity or changes in climate

distributed energy—the generation of energy by small-scale facilities located close to where the energy is used; can be an alternative or enhancement to the centralized power grid

divestment—a movement that aims to pressure investors to get rid of investments that support the fossil fuel industry

eco-anxiety—See *climate anxiety*

ecological footprint—a measure of the quantity of nature (e.g., timber, minerals, water, fossil fuels) consumed by a person, group of people or economy every year; see also *carbon footprint*

ecosystem services—the direct and indirect benefits of healthily functioning ecosystems, including provisioning (such as supplying food and water), regulating (such as controlling climate and disease), supporting (forming soil, producing oxygen and cycling nutrients) and cultural services (recreational and spiritual contributions)

extractivism—the removal of natural resources for sale, unprocessed, on world markets

fake news—false or inaccurate information spread deliberately through traditional or social media

fossil fuels—nonrenewable fuels such as coal, oil and natural gas that are formed over millions of years from prehistoric plants and animals that died and were buried by rock

free trade—international trade in goods and services without the usual regulatory barriers, such as tariffs, taxes and quotas

global warming potential (GWP)—the amount of energy one ton of a gas will absorb over a given period relative to one ton of carbon dioxide. GWP is 1 for CO_2. The higher the GWP, the more the given gas warms the atmosphere compared to carbon dioxide.

globalization—the process by which trade, communication and cultural exchange make the world more interconnected and interdependent

greenhouse gases—gases in the atmosphere, such as carbon dioxide, methane and nitrous oxide, that absorb and emit infrared energy, which is heat

gross domestic product (GDP)—the monetary value of all goods and services produced by a country in a certain period of time, generally reported annually

heat sink—a reservoir, such as the ocean, that absorbs heat

imperialism—the policy of one nation extending its governing power over another nation, often over Indigenous Peoples; see also *colonialism*

individualism—a doctrine that emphasizes the individual, self-reliance and personal independence

Industrial Revolution—the change from a farming and craft economy to an industrial manufacturing economy that started in Britain in the late 1700s and spread to other areas of the world

infrared—a form of radiant energy from the sun that is invisible but felt as heat

internally displaced person (IDP)—a person who has been forced from their home by conflict, violence, natural disasters, development projects or climate change but remains within their home country

intersectionality—how people's experiences of oppression are shaped by their race, class, gender, ethnicity and sexuality

moral authority—trustworthiness to make right and good decisions

neoliberalism—an economic policy that aims to transfer control of the economy from the public sector to the private sector; it favors free-market capitalism, free trade, economic growth and limited government interference in markets

net-zero emissions—when the annual amount of carbon dioxide emissions into Earth's atmosphere is equal to the annual amount removed from the atmosphere by natural ecosystems

paleoclimates—past climates, which scientists reconstruct and study by using proxies (materials created in the past), such as tree rings, ice cores and ocean-bottom sediments

passive home—a house so energy-efficient that it requires little or no mechanical cooling or heating and as such has a low ecological footprint

permaculture—a set of ethical and ecological principles by which farming, building and living practices function in harmony with nature

refugee—a person who has crossed a border into another country to flee war, violence, conflict or persecution and is unable or unwilling to return owing to reasonable fear of being persecuted; refugees are protected by international law

rewilding—conservation focused on restoring biodiversity and ecosystem health in large, often interconnected areas of wild land and/or water by protecting them and reintroducing large predators, particularly carnivores and other ecologically important (keystone) species

sacrifice zone—a geographic area, often located in low-income or minority communities, that has been permanently impaired by environmental damage or economic disinvestment, often through locally unwanted land-use decisions

steady-state economy—an economy that balances population and consumption in order to stay within ecological limits

supply chain—the network of people, resources and technology required to produce an item from raw materials and get it to consumers

swales—in permaculture design, shallow trenches dug along the land's contour, with a raised bank on the downhill side, to retain water and reduce erosion

thermal expansion—the tendency of a material to increase in volume as its temperature increases

thermal inertia—a measure of a material's responsiveness to changes in temperature

tipping points—thresholds beyond which certain effects or changes become unstoppable

urban heat island effect—the tendency of cities to be warmer than surrounding land, due to the prevalence of heat-absorbing surfaces (roads and buildings), the lack of green vegetation and the concentration of heat-emitting sources such as vehicles and heating and cooling devices

wildland-urban interface—the area where homes and related infrastructure meet or are interspersed with areas of wild vegetation, making them more vulnerable to natural wildfire

RESOURCES

PRINT

Berners-Lee, Mike. *There Is No Planet B: A Handbook for the Make or Break Years.* Cambridge University Press, 2019.

Bigelow, Bill, and Tim Swinehart (editors). *A People's Curriculum for the Earth.* Rethinking Schools, 2014.

Dauncey, Guy. *The Climate Challenge: 101 Solutions to Global Warming.* New Society Publishers, 2009.

Eisenstein, Charles. *Climate: A New Story.* North Atlantic Books, 2018.

Ernman, Malena, Greta Thunberg, Svante Thunberg and Beata Ernman. *Our House Is On Fire: Scenes from a Family and a Planet in Crisis.* Penguin Books, 2020.

Extinction Rebellion. *This Is Not a Drill: An Extinction Rebellion Handbook.* Penguin UK, 2019.

Holmgren, David. *RetroSuburbia: The Downshifter's Guide to a Resilient Future.* Melliodora Publishing, 2018.

Jahren, Hope. *The Story of More: How We Got to Climate Change and Where to Go From Here.* Vintage, 2020.

Kimmerer, Robin Wall. *Braiding Sweetgrass: Indigenous Wisdom, Scientific Knowledge and the Teachings of Plants.* Milkweed Editions, 2013.

Klein, Naomi with Rebecca Stefoff. *How to Change Everything: A Young Human's Guide to Protecting the Planet and Each Other.* Atheneum Books for Young Readers, 2021.

Lloyd, Saci. *The Carbon Diaries 2015* (2005) and *The Carbon Diaries 2017* (2009). Hodder Children's Books.

Margolin, Jamie. *Youth to Power: Your Voice and How to Use It.* Hatchette Go, 2020.

McKibben, Bill. *Oil and Honey: The Education of an Unlikely Activist.* St. Martin's Press, 2014.

Nakate, Vanessa. *A Bigger Picture: My Fight to Bring a New African Voice to the Climate Crisis.* Houghton Mifflin, 2021.

Powers, Richard. *The Overstory.* W.W. Norton, 2018.

Raygorodetsky, Gleb. *The Archipelago of Hope: Wisdom and Resilience from the Edge of Climate Change.* Pegasus Books, 2017.

Thunberg, Greta. *No One Is Too Small to Make a Difference.* Penguin Books, 2019.

ONLINE

350.org

A Matter of Degrees podcast: podcastaddict.com/podcast/3128046

ChangeX: changex.org

Conceivable Future: conceivablefuture.org

Earth Guardians: earthguardians.org

Extinction Rebellion: rebellion.earth

Fridays For Future: fridaysforfuture.org

Global Weirding with Katharine Hayhoe:
youtube.com/c/GlobalWeirdingwithKatharineHayhoe/featured

Good Grief Network: goodgriefnetwork.org

International Indigenous Youth Council: indigenousyouth.org

La Via Campesina: viacampesina.org/en/who-are-we/youth

Our Children's Trust: ourchildrenstrust.org

Project Drawdown: drawdown.org

Stop Ecocide: stopecocide.earth

Sunrise Movement: sunrisemovement.org

Transition Network: transitionnetwork.org

United Nations Declaration on the Rights of Indigenous Peoples (UNDRIP): un.org/
development/desa/indigenouspeoples/declaration-on-the-rights-of-indigenous-peoples.html

Zero Hour: thisiszerohour.org

Links to external resources are for personal and/or educational use only and are
provided in good faith without any express or implied warranty. There is no guarantee
given as to the accuracy or currency of any individual item. The author and publisher
provide links as a service to readers. This does not imply any endorsement by the author
or publisher of any of the content accessed through these links.

For a complete list of references, visit the page for this book on our website (orcabook.com).

PHOTO CREDITS

INDEX

*Page numbers in **bold** indicate an image caption.*